Weeping May Endure for a Night

A Spiritual Journey

By C. Albert Snyder, M.D., F.A.C.S.

Weeping may endure for a night,
but joy comes in the morning.
Ps. 30:5

*For Michele with my best wishes
wishing you God's best.*

Al Snyder

Job 19:25-27

PRESS

Endorsements

Weeping May Endure for a Night provides a rare glimpse of life and faith through the well-traveled perspective of a medical missionary surgeon. Here you will find a delightful collection of stories—a blend of fascinating medical experiences, profound insights, and commonsense wisdom, all woven together with humor and grace. Dr. Snyder's own transparent faith journey will be an encouragement to many a reader. God's grace and truth can be found everywhere, and Al Snyder helps us discover it in the oddest places!

—Pastor Mark Van Valin, senior pastor,
Spring Arbor Free Methodist Church

Al writes from his heart. Read and expect tears and laughter, insight and penetrating truth. Walk with Al Snyder through the "dark night of the soul," in the throes of crisis, while living and worshipping the Lord. Anticipate rewards—"aha!" moments, family joys, discoveries of liberating life and love. I commend Dr. Snyder's book, seasoned by experiences and written with a sensitive pen. Read. Loan. Hang on to it for reading over and again.

—Dr. Donald E. Demaray,
senior professor of biblical preaching,
Asbury Theological Seminary

Dedication

This book is dedicated to my beloved wife, Louise.
She has traveled with me to Africa more times
than we can count. She has stayed by my side
through sickness and health, for richer and poorer,
for better and for worse. It has been better
than I could have dreamed when we both took those
vows at age twenty-one.

Who can find a virtuous wife?
For her worth is far above rubies.
The heart of her husband safely trusts her;
So he will have no lack of gain
She does him good and not evil
All the days of her life.
Prov. 31:10-12

Acknowledgements

I am indebted to many people for their help in bringing this book to publication:

Vera Bethel, who has given much of her time in editing, proofreading, and providing valuable suggestions.

Walter Pettifor, for help in editing and proofreading.

The Spring Arbor Creative Writing Class, for valuable suggestions on most of the essays that appear in this book.

Dan Runyon, professor at Spring Arbor University, who gave valuable suggestions and guidance.

Karen Parsons of Spring Arbor University Library.

Betty Videto, social science secretary at Spring Arbor University, who did a great job consolidating the essays done on several different word processors into one manuscript using Microsoft Word.

Light and Life Communications, for permitting me to borrow several pages on depression from my previous book, *On a Hill Far Away*.

The Central Africa Healthcare Organization (CAHO) Board of Directors, for permitting me to publish this in affiliation with the organization.

Attorney Steven Rick, for valuable advice.

The Free Methodist Foundation, for permitting CAHO to function under its auspices and for allowing its personnel to help with technical assistance, specifically Danette Brandymore and Ruth Rupert, in preparing the manuscript.

Pastor Mark Van Valin, senior pastor of the Spring Arbor Free Methodist Church, who read the manuscript and encouraged me to publish it. He also provided an endorsement for the cover.

Dr. Donald Demaray, professor emeritus at Asbury Theological Seminary, who read the manuscript, encouraged me to publish it, and contributed an endorsement.

Dr. Elmore Clyde, longtime friend, missionary colleague, and former director of Free Methodist World Missions. Elmore and his wife, Arlene, read essays, made suggestions, and encouraged me along the way. Their advice is always good. Elmore has kindly contributed the foreword to this book.

Table of Contents

Foreword

By Dr. Elmore Clyde

One of the many blessings of overseas missionary service is the building of lasting friendships with colleagues. My friendship with Dr. C. Albert Snyder and his family began in 1962 while he was serving in South Africa. He writes with amazing candor of this time in "My Dark Night of the Soul."

For my wife and me, the nature of our friendship has always been on a first-name basis, although when talking about him to others I refer to him as "Dr. Al." This was true even during our years of involvement in missions administration. It was then we developed a deep appreciation for his keen insights and the fact that he always told it like it is. His practical wisdom was of great value when grappling with administrative issues. This was especially so in matters pertaining to the national church because of the high respect the church leadership had for him.

As you join with Dr. Al on his spiritual journey, you will be blessed and challenged as you get a glimpse of who he really is. You will see at least some of what I have experienced through our friendship. He has a strong faith in our sovereign Lord. There is a sincere dedication to medical missions and to serving others. His love for family is a model for all.

As you read the section titled Observations Along the Way, you soon will become aware of his unusual gift of seeing beyond the mere facts of an event to the practical spiritual lessons that are often overlooked. These observations give evidence of keen practical, theological, and missiological insights.

The book ends, as it begins, with another example of his candor in coming to grips with a personal struggle and the reality of God's love. Join with me in praising God for His amazing love as revealed in and through the pen of Dr. C. Albert Snyder.

Dr. Elmore Clyde, M.Div., doctor of divinity, is a former missionary to South Africa and past executive director of Free Methodist World Missions.

Introduction

S ome things sprout and take root without our knowing when they began to germinate—the crabgrass along my front walk for example. I cannot imagine how it got started. Though crabgrass is an irritation, often we find happy surprises, especially around old neglected buildings: some beautiful roses, tiger lilies, or hollyhocks holding their own, smiling up among the weeds, saying, "Good morning. We are still here."

This book has evolved, germinated for a long time. It finally took root. I don't want it to fall into the crabgrass category; I hope it smiles up at you like hidden flowers saying, "You can find joy in the morning. Weeping never lasts forever." There is always hope, even if you are struggling with depression or just paddling through life, trying to keep afloat.

Two things have motivated this writing. First, after writing *On a Hill Far Away*, with a short account about depression, many people called or wrote to say how much it helped them, or they asked for a copy for a friend. That made me feel an obligation to share the whole story as it now appears in the first chapter, "My Dark Night of the Soul." It has been painful to do this. Nobody wants to be unmasked or stand in public in their underwear.

The second reason is that for the last few years I have been sending out essays written about life experiences. These have accompanied our Central Africa newsletter—"The CAHO CHRONICLE." The feedback has surprised me; many readers asked to have them put together in a book. They have begun to pile up to a point where they will either languish in my files to die with me, or be bound together and made available to others.

These essays, although drawn from medical missionary experiences, are for the most part related to life experiences that we all face and that involve such concepts as courage, integrity, providence, standing up for right, and so forth.

The final essay, "My Journey into Light," is my favorite. Writing this has articulated for me how enormous God's love is. As I described this and meditated upon it, my legalistic, stark, cold, disciplined Christian life began to warm, glow, and grow brighter. My joy in being a Christian became so much more exciting and real. I felt I must share it.

In looking over the manuscript, things began to come into focus as a spiritual journey. Part One starts out as a bumpy, dangerous road where I almost fall off the cliff. The journey gets pleasant as I get through that trip and evolves to something much better as I travel along supported by my mentor, Dr. Charlie Robb. Along this part of the road, I realize how indispensable to my recovery is the love of my wife, Louise.

Part Two is best described as lessons learned or Observations Along the Way.

Part Three is the great conclusion of this spiritual journey. I finally discover that God is love. It is said that when someone asked theologian Karl Barth what was the most profound theological truth he ever discovered, he replied, "Jesus loves me, this I know, For the Bible tells me so."

The most appropriate title I could think of comes from Psalm 30:5: "Weeping may endure for a night, but joy comes in the morning. Hence my title, *Weeping May Endure for a Night: A Spiritual Journey.*

—C. Albert Snyder

Part One:

Every Road Has Its Bumps

My Dark Night of the Soul

The spirit of a man will sustain him in sickness,
but who can bear a broken spirit?
Proverbs 18:14

I am about to recount a story known in its entirety to only four people. Two of the four—Dr. David Stewart and Dr. Stuart Bergsma—are now deceased; that leaves Louise and me. I share it for one reason. It might help guide another person who is groping through a "dark night of the soul" experience. It might be a beam of light from the shore for someone who is lost as they sail through life alone. It might help one of my own children or grandchildren who had inherited the same traits and chemical imbalances that course through the veins of many of the Zahniser clan from which my mother hailed. I refer to the anxiety and depression combination, the bugaboo of our times. For years it was my Siamese twin, another self that I tried not to reveal. Something I tolerated, hoping that no one noticed it.

I grew up thinking it would be a disgrace to be seen weeping. No man should ever be afraid. The "tough guy" posture came from my dad's side. The Snyders were natural fighters, standing unafraid, chin up, shoulders back, chest out, belly in, jaw out, daring anyone to take a swing at it. Somehow, I survived more than two years in the army, made it through college, got married, started a family, and was in medical school before I ever "crashed." I thought all my anxieties, low moments, and struggles were normal. Three weeks into medical school, knowing no one, belonging to no fraternity or group of Christian brothers, I crashed for the first time in my life. I had tried to learn everything almost word for word out of my textbooks. This was not working. I did not know that almost everyone else also felt as if they were trying to drink out of a fire hose, as each new day a torrent of learning gushed forth from professors who had written the books. If I failed it would disgrace my father, an alumnus and former faculty member who had specialized in orthopedics. Many of the professors were his friends. I panicked, I could not sleep, I did not feel like eating. What to do? Quit, get out before they throw me out—that was my decision.

I called home and told my mother my solution. "Never," she insisted.

"But I can't eat, I can't sleep. I don't know what to do," I said.

"Don't eat, don't sleep, get up, and study," she persisted.

I had already stopped going to classes but had not yet gone to the dean's office. My dad sent some sleeping pills. My mother called one of the "saints" in our church, and together they began to pray and beseech heaven on my behalf. My dad was crushed but strangely did not come on strong. But the parental pressure, with all its power, was released. With my supportive wife standing by, I began to knuckle down as I learned one of the biggest lessons in life. If you are going to succeed, you must be willing to fail.

Somehow, I threw off my fear and despondency; I got to know some Christians and other friends in class. When the semester ended, I had made it and gotten into the second semester. Looking back, as I have gone through many other tough times, I can see that the difference between success and failure is refusing to quit. One more stroke, one more blow, one more step can be the crucial move that pulls us through. The light at the end of the tunnel may be just around the next dark corner.

It was my senior year, and graduation was approaching. One beautiful day in May, it was balmy outside; lilacs, iris, and tulips were everywhere. Gorgeous! On my surgery rotation, my work for the day was done. I was counting on getting off early, so called my wife to pick me up at the back of the hospital where the road winds up the hill from the Huron River. My resident said I could go but told me to first look at the patient in room 312, who had shot himself in the head in an attempted suicide. I walked down the hall and peered into the room. There, alone, lying on the stretcher, was a young man in his twenties. He was in overalls, a big dressing pad obscuring the top of his head. Big blue eyes, open, fixed, and motionless, stared blankly like the glass eyes of a mounted hunting trophy. He was still breathing, but nobody was attending him. No treatment was possible. I lifted the surgical pad and peered under. The top of his head from the hairline back was gone, shot away, and only mushy brain material was visible. He had been wheeled into the room to die. No family members were with him; perhaps they had not yet been notified. The only lesson I could think the resident wanted me to learn was how sad, how helpless you can feel in medicine. Or perhaps he just thought I needed to be toughened to the realities of a life of practicing medicine.

I left the hospital and walked outside to meet Louise. The day was warm, the sunshine and gentle wind comforting, the birds singing. Ah, spring, the most wonderful time of the year. I opened the car door and got in. Louise was exhilarated, her spirit radiant. I was trying to recover from what I had just seen. I described it to her.

Aghast, she asked, "Why would anyone want to kill himself on a beautiful day like this?"

That brought a laugh as I asked, "You mean some nasty, cold, rainy day you might be able to understand it? Does it depend on the weather?"

Suicide had always been a terrifying thing for me. My mother had the idea, which I think comes from Catholic teaching, that suicide is a mortal sin, because God said, "Thou shalt not kill." Suicide is killing, murder. Thus you would not only lose your life, but you would also lose your soul. I have since come to think differently about this. God is love, God is merciful, and someone suffering from clinical depression can lose normal reasoning ability.

I went into my internship and then proceeded into a surgical residency. After two years of this I felt compelled to answer the call of my early years to become a medical missionary. We were appointed to Burundi in Africa.

We moved to Brussels for language study, then to Antwerp to study tropical medicine—in French. I completed that program in February 1957, and we prepared to leave for Burundi, Africa, just six weeks after our fourth son, Daniel, entered our family. During the time in Belgium and while serving in Burundi, I began experiencing periods of increased anxiety. I thought this was within the realm of normal, and I managed to keep others from knowing it. I kept a poker face; I feigned an air of confidence when I performed surgery or treated other missionaries. I was especially stressed when I had to care for or deliver babies for missionary colleagues.

Back in the U.S., I returned to surgical residency, just four years to the day after I had left to go to Africa. With all the support of those working with me or over me as instructors, I had worked in a consistent environment. I did not experience any real anxiety during those years. (Years later, I made an observation about how to live without anxiety—don't do anything risky). But a risky lifestyle was what I chose, and we readied to leave again for Africa.

As the time approached to leave with four school-age children, we began to wonder if it was stupid to go out of the country in such turbulent times. Many of the nations of Africa were entering periods of instability. Should we wait awhile and let the world settle down?

As I wrestled with what was the right thing and what was the wise thing to do, I began to experience great anxiety again. The decision to follow the Lord was firm, but what was the Lord telling us to do? This was in 1962; the Congo crisis was heating up. (In 1964, Dr. Paul Carlson was killed in Stanleyville, Congo. One of the British doctors who had taken the tropical medicine course just ahead of me in Antwerp was also killed, along with his entire family, in the Congo). Would Rwanda and Burundi go the way of Congo? Such was the political climate in Central Africa in those days.

While in the midst of this turmoil and doing a rotation on the anesthesia service, I received a long-distance call from our mission board. It was from the general director, Dr. Byron Lamson.

He asked, "Would you consider going to South Africa as the doctor at our Greenville Mission Hospital? Could you come down tomorrow to discuss it with me and the area director?"

I answered, "Sure," and thought, "Wow, is God coming up with a different plan?" This was tempting. It would be more pleasant and safe in a country still ruled by whites, a country with lots of colleagues who had children going to public schools. It seemed like a miraculous answer to the dilemma we were facing.

The next day, the meeting with the mission executives resulted in a complete change of plans. We felt very excited and eager to have this solution that was not of our making, so we chose to say yes. But I never felt totally at peace about it, even though there was another doctor filling my old post in Burundi. Reason told me this is what I should do. It was God's answer to our family problems, but my heart and my emotions told me I was taking the easy way out. I was betraying my missionary colleagues, my African friends in Burundi. I was walking out on my first love. I was a coward, avoiding danger.

Had our assignment to South Africa ended happily, I am sure I would have felt we had been entirely in God's will. But quite the contrary: it ended in disaster!

The doctor whom I was to replace had nothing against me personally, but he was determined the mission board was not going to dislodge him from the hospital he founded and considered *his*. Just days before we were to leave the U.S., he sent a cablegram saying that a medical license for me had not been obtained and that I should be sure I could practice medicine in South Africa before coming. But our mission director told me to go as scheduled. He was sure it would all work out. We were to go to England by ship and after a few days sail from Southampton on the Union Castle Line and then for fourteen days to Durban. These long days on the ship, with little activity and much time for thought, were not particularly happy. I kept wondering what we were getting into.

For years people had been predicting some sort of apocalypse, a time when white rule would end with terrible fighting and bloodshed. Sometimes, adverse news about isolated incidents in South Africa would pop up and were disturbing. What was the situation with regard to my license to practice medicine? During those long days aboard the ship, anxiety would descend upon me. Where was this all leading?

The ship, part of the British mail system, stopped at many ports. We were allowed off to visit Cape Town, certainly one of the most beautiful ports in the world, with its view of Table Mountain. Here a gorgeous basket of flowers was delivered to our stateroom from the doctor I was to replace. "Welcome to South Africa," the card read. That was interesting; had he changed his mind? Were we really welcome? Maybe this would be a positive adventure yet.

A few days later, the entire missionary group met us at Durban. We were to have dinner together, and then the doctor and his wife would take us to Greenville mission station where the hospital was located. But it was strange. Following lunch and some brief visiting we were hustled off in his new Ford Galaxy sedan; we thought we were on our way for the long trip to Greenville mission. But instead of immediately driving out of Durban, we drove around town while the doctor made a bunch of stops and ran various errands. I wondered why we could not have stayed with the other missionaries to visit, get acquainted, and ask questions. From that moment everything became more and more perplexing. We were to stay in the doctor's large house, and since their children were away at school, we were given two bedrooms for ourselves.

At every meal we heard more about the history of the South Africa mission work, the hospital, and how he, having been born in South Africa, could understand the problems of the mission, the hospital, and the very delicate political situation in the country. He believed there was a conspiracy to get him out of there. He blamed the area director for the entire mess.

But in many ways, Dr. Lowell Rice was a genius. Probably ten to fifteen years my senior, he did have an understanding of South Africa, the Zulu language, and the people. He was an electrician, mechanic, and a builder but a very out-of-date medical doctor. Being around him and listening to him, I began to like the guy and felt sorry for him. I asked to meet with the mission executive committee to discuss what I was to do in the situation I had been put in.

The doctor was not on the executive committee, so I freely presented the dilemma as I saw it. I asked them to request the home board to let the doctor stay on for the time being, and I would work with him. They agreed, and I began to see a change in the doctor's attitude.

Dr. Rice had previously telephoned a Dr. Barnhart, head of the medical council and licensing in Pretoria, and put me on the phone to hear him say, "Dr. Snyder, I have to inform you that you are not licensed in this country, and you are not allowed to perform one medical act." Now Dr. Rice told me he would go to Pretoria and personally present my case.

In the meantime, we got settled in their walkout basement— our living room, dining room, and kitchen, plus the two bedrooms upstairs. In the daytime, I occupied myself with driving the mission water truck to a reservoir on a nearby white trader's land, start a pump, fill the tank, drive back to Greenville station, and discharge the water into the mission reservoir. While waiting around, I studied Zulu.

When Dr. Rice returned from Pretoria, he assured me that my license would now come through. I began to take night calls. Frequently, I was called out to tend nasty machete or knife wounds. Sewing these up would be the only surgery I ever got to do in South Africa. About three weeks later a letter addressed to me arrived from Pretoria. The mail had been deposited at the hospital, so I took the letter and started walking to the house to share it with Louise. Part way to the house I could not bear the suspense, so opened it.

It read: "The medical council of South Africa has approved your practicing medicine in South Africa, provided your practice is restricted to Greenville Mission Hospital and a doctor trained in South Africa is always in charge of the hospital."

Some very unchristian things began to go through my mind. I realized then that it had been a chess game from the beginning. I realized how much pent-up hostility I was repressing. I could see that Dr. Rice was as wary of me as I was of him and had me checkmated. I was almost trembling as I shared the letter with Louise.

Here we were, Dr. and Mrs. Rice and Louise and I, in an impossible situation devised by mission executives who were not facing the problem head-on. Instead, they came up with a plan, one that did not work. We became the victims. Louise and I both liked the Rices well enough, and they did not personally dislike us, except as we represented the mission board that the doctor perceived was about to separate him from his lifelong work. So, we determined to get to work and hope for a happier solution to evolve, but it didn't. Certainly, the entire saga was as frustrating and upsetting to the Rices as to us.

My colleague's confidence in me began to strengthen a little. Until then, his trust in me had been limited to my taking the night calls. I would go out for maternity deliveries, which were not numerous, and for lacerations and injuries from drunken brawls among the Xhosa people. The latter incidents were fairly frequent.

Now things had changed. I was left in charge of hospital work for a few days every now and then when my colleague had some business to tend to in Durban. His way of seeing patients was to sit in his clinic, with his nurse/wife by his side, and see each patient individually, beginning in midmorning and finishing some time after dark. Coming as I did from Central Africa where the patient load ran into the hundreds each day, that was not the system I was used to. Further, in Central Africa, we had the philosophy that a national should be taught to take the missionary's place if and when it became necessary. Dr. Rice, being a white South African, had different ideas. In fact, he was steeped in the apartheid philosophy. At the same time, he loved the Africans, spoke Zulu fluently, and was loved and revered as the "Big Bwana."

My first day in charge of the clinic I looked at the thirty or so patients waiting for me and said to Miss Mary, an American nurse with long experience in South Africa, that I was going to work things differently. I asked her to screen them and bring their charts to me, and I would choose which ones I thought needed to be seen by a doctor. She could treat the others and call me for any problems. We were finished long before nightfall.

As I looked over the charts, I began to notice that nearly every one of Dr. Rice's patients had received numerous medications, plus a shot of penicillin. I could not believe what I was seeing. I pored over twenty-seven previous charts and found that every patient, except one with a fractured collarbone, had received a packet of pills, a powder, and a shot of penicillin. Wow! No wonder our home board thought Dr. Rice needed a refresher course in the U.S.

When my colleague returned and checked the charts of patients I had seen, he came to me privately. "There is something I need to tell you," he said. "These patients are used to always receiving a supply of pills, a packet of powder, and an injection. They expect to pay five shillings for this. If they receive anything less they will stop coming. I have spent years building up this practice, and I can't allow this to happen."

I felt trapped. I could not do this for conscience' sake, even if I were willing to submit to this kind of domination. The days ahead began to look dark. I managed to get through a couple more clinics, straining my conscience to the limit. But it became increasingly apparent that the only way I could survive at this hospital was for us to separate our areas of work. Since I was a surgeon and he had little knowledge or experience in this field, I started to push Dr. Rice to begin providing surgery. When I discussed this with him, he replied that the law in South Africa required three doctors be present if one was to operate—one as surgeon, one as assistant, and one to give anesthesia.

"Could we get a colleague from another mission hospital to come once a week?" I asked. "That would make three doctors present."

He replied, "It might be possible, but practically it would be difficult to work out the details."

Once again I was stymied. Could this mess have been God's will? Or was I reaping the results of doing my own thing? Was I a Jonah on his way to Tarshish? I didn't know, but intermittent spells of darkness began to descend. And inside the belly of a whale it could not have been much darker. I began to feel guilty for not having gone back to Central Africa. The whole situation began to be a nightmare, and one with personal recriminations. I began to take it out on myself.

Somewhere in my mind was lurking the horror of a young internist at Butterworth Hospital who had taken his own life. Earl Schumaker was one of the nicest people on the hospital staff, bright, friendly, helpful—a congenital nice guy. Why had he done this? From the time I heard about it I could not understand it. He seemed like someone who loved his family and cared for others. The idea burned into my mind that for some people this was inevitable, something they could not help. I could never quite get over it. It lay deep in my own mental horror chamber. It became a fear like some people have of cancer or a heart attack. This, fueled by the impossible situation I had been thrust into with no seeming answer to my dilemma, gnawed at me day and night.

One day after Dr. Rice had visited Durban he shared a disaster story.

"You know, when we are in Durban we always attend a certain evangelical church. They are good spiritual people. I just heard that the Sunday school superintendent has taken his own life. I just can't believe it!"

This story pierced my mind, and I felt weak and shaky as I thought, "This happens to Christians?"

Anxiety and depression began to dominate my life from then on. Sometimes less, sometimes more, sometimes with unbearable mental anguish and pain. Not having enough work to keep me busy made it more difficult. The joy went out of my life. Guilt and melancholy moved into its place. My wonderful wife remained calm and supportive.

I began to write home about my exasperation. I could see there was no answer to the difficult situation I was working in. I phoned the director of missions; he encouraged me to hang on.

Then he said, "You know what your father said to me? He said, 'Nothing ever gets better by running from it.'" That was not much comfort. It was apparent he did not have an answer, and it was hard for him to accept the failure of his plan.

We decided to get away for a while and went to Durban. Someone suggested we drive up to southern Rhodesia and visit Victoria Falls—take a vacation, get away. We left Durban in an effort to do this, but traveling in a strange land with my family was not a good solution. How can you get away from something that is inside your own head? Louise agreed with me that we abandon the trip. When things would get really nasty, I would retch and vomit. Not sleeping, not eating, living in mental anguish in an impossible situation made every five minutes seem like an hour. Nights were interminable.

Fortunately, I did have enough sense to realize this was not normal, that I was sick, just as sick as someone with a headache and fever. But for that, people can take aspirin or use an ice pack. Depression is a nightmare, along with insomnia, feeling like having the flu with a high fever, combined with fatigue and hopelessness. If hell is anything like depression, I want to stay away from there. I had much support from other missionaries, especially Elmore Clyde, who has remained one of my lifelong friends. And my wife stood by my side, never criticizing, always sympathetic.

But what should we do? Where should we turn? Finally, it seemed obvious: go for help. Rather than running from the problem, I decided to run for help.

It was the end of February, and a snowstorm prevented our landing in New York. We were diverted to Montreal and lodged there for the night before continuing on to Michigan. My immediate goal was to contact my missionary friend from Burundi days, Dr. David Stewart, now practicing psychiatry in Louisville. We left our boys with family and drove down to his house. He would not be home for a couple of hours, and the wait seemed endless. Louise talked to Laura Stewart, and I walked the neighborhood. Then there was supper and an attempt to be friendly as usual. Finally, at about 8 p.m. David and I sat down in his study, and I unloaded.

He heard me out and then said, "Al, you need to be hospitalized." That was the bad news. The good news was that someone else was now taking charge. Just knowing that gave me some comfort.

"But where and what hospital?" I queried.

"Here in Louisville," he replied.

"If I have to be in a hospital, I want to be home where my wife and family can be in familiar circumstances and the kids in school. Let's contact Dr. Stuart Bergsma," I suggested.

Stuart Bergsma was an acquaintance and former missionary, now a psychiatrist practicing in Grand Rapids. Dave called him at home, and I was able to hear one side of their conversation, all the while guessing what was being said on the other end.

The following afternoon, back in Grand Rapids, I had my first consultation with Dr. Bergsma and then was admitted to Pine Rest Christian Hospital. Immediately it became a refuge, but the journey back to wellness turned out to be long, painful, and arduous.

In many ways this hospitalization was a defeat and a humiliation, but I had an example in a much-admired surgeon friend. He had been hospitalized for narcotics addiction (and I am sure depression), sought psychotherapy, and fought his way back to a point where he became chief of surgery. He had even done an appendectomy on me a few years before. Close friends remembered how he had driven to the university once or twice a month for a long period while undergoing psychotherapy. I admired that kind of person, one who recognized something was wrong and set about to get it fixed. He was an outstanding, skilled surgeon, and one who was very kind. I aspired to be like him. Over the years I have concluded that people judge you by what you are today and how you treat them, and not by what happened in the past.

After my first consultation Dr. Bergsma suggested electroshock therapy. I did not relish the idea. He decided to first consult a colleague. So, the next day I went through the whole story again, and the consultant advised the same treatment.

Each Monday for six weeks I was pre-medicated for an anesthetic and rolled up to the room, where I would be given an intravenous anesthetic with a muscle relaxant to keep me from breaking any bones while undergoing the convulsion. I would wake up in a bed later. It was harder for me, since in medical school I had watched patients undergoing these treatments.

The rest of the days were occupied with "busy work"—activities like woodworking shop, sports, and other programs. All the time I was medicated and would meet with Dr. Bergsma each day, and we would talk. He would listen and make helpful comments. I kept a journal and notes as though I was in training, all the time trying to get to the bottom of my problem. To my surprise this was not going to be a psychoanalysis and rebuilding a new healthy psyche, but the approach seemed to be one of recognizing where we are today and what can we do to face tomorrow successfully, learning what ways I had been perceiving things wrongly, and how I could think differently. I need to change my reflex way of thinking.

Another great surprise awaited me. I had concluded that my career as a surgeon was finished—that there was no way, with my disposition, that I could ever become a successful surgeon. I still hoped to return to being a missionary. But, as time went on, what I was hearing from Dr. B was that I would assuredly get better, that I must establish myself as a surgeon, and pass the board of surgery examinations. Perhaps in the future, maybe after five years, we would talk about a missionary career again.

Spring was beginning to show itself; the trees were budding, the flowers blooming. Our boys were back in the schools they had previously attended. Louise was my anchor. She would come by most afternoons, and we would go for drives in a car borrowed from my parents. Daily life was bearable. Suicidal thoughts were far away, but one day in one of the sessions with Dr. B we discussed this. I hoped he would say it was obviously just a fear; instead, he said that while the risk was low the temptations were real. That day I took an emotional nosedive. I went to my room and sobbed. How could I be so awful, so unchristian, so self-centered, so thoughtless of my family? How could I be such a wretch? How could I face life? The word suicide haunted me. I avoided reading newspapers, listening to, or watching the news. Whenever I heard or read the word suicide I crashed emotionally.

After six weeks, in April 1963 I was discharged.

As I left, an older, experienced male nurse said to me, "Just remember you will have good days and bad days; we all have them." His words stuck with me. That simple piece of advice kept me going through many bad days that lay ahead. I was to see Dr. B once a week, and he was always available by phone. He marveled at how quickly I had come out of the deep depression. But once I left the hospital the hardest part of my recovery began. I was on a mood elevator and a tranquilizer that helped me, the latter especially for sleep. Dr. Bergsma urged me to keep busy. I did this initially by refinishing furniture.

Social situations were difficult. One time after being in a group for dinner at my mother's house, she mentioned to me how I should try to be more cheerful and not so tied up inside myself.

In spite of my love for my mother, I thought, "Mom, if you only knew what was going on inside me you wouldn't make such a suggestion."

People are so unthinking in the remarks they make around someone who is suffering inside, and Mom did not mean to be anything but helpful. A parting word of advice Dr. Bergsma had given me as I was discharged was this: "Don't share your problems with many others. Restrict that to just your wife and perhaps one other confidant." Church sermons, rather than being uplifting, often would throw me into despair.

One day I had gone for a scheduled consultation with Dr. Bergsma. As I was driving home the red flashers and bells signaled me to stop for an approaching train roaring down the track. I stopped and waited and then broke out into a sweat as I thought how simple it would be to unfasten my seatbelt and drive into its path. Of course, this put me into a nosedive again. At my folks' home there were hunting guns around and drawers full of ammunition. These, and even sharp knives, were upsetting to me.

Someone would probably ask, "But where was God in all this? Where was the God you trusted?"

Fortunately, someone had told me that in depression the spiritual lights often go out. I have to say from an emotional standpoint that this is true. I could not feel His presence. Intellectually, I blindly held on. It was a "dark night of the soul" experience. I could find little comfort from Scripture. My daily devotions consisted of reading just one chapter from the Psalms—especially Psalm 34, in which verse 4 reads, "I sought the Lord, and He heard me and delivered me from all my fears." And verse 6, "This poor man cried out, and the Lord heard him, and saved him out of all his troubles." And verse 7, "The angel of the Lord encamps all around those who fear Him, and delivers them." Often in my darkest hours I would, by sheer determination, quote Job's affirmation: "Though He slay me, yet will I trust Him."

Some years later I found some apt words spoken by the apostle Paul in Acts 27:20. "Now when neither sun nor stars appeared for many days, and no small tempest beat on us, all hope that we would be saved was finally given up." And verse 29 seemed so descriptive of what I had done in those days: "Then, fearing lest we should run aground on the rocks, they dropped four anchors from the stem, and prayed for day to come." For me, day after day, night after night, I just hung on, trusting Dr. B's words: "You will get better." And blindly believing Psalm 34, which assures us that God hears, delivers, and heals. Slowly, the good times became more frequent and longer. The down times became less frequent and shorter. And mood fluctuations were less intense in frequency and depth.

V. Raymond Edman, former president of Wheaton College, used to admonish students that "It's always too soon to quit." One more blow may win the fight, one more minute, hour, or day may bring light or understanding or a solution or success. Or just standing still and waiting, we may see the sun peeping over the mountains.

Even before I had left Pine Rest Christian Hospital I began to hear indirectly that there were those who would like me to join their practice of surgery. Since I was somewhat sequestered by being in a hospital some distance from the general medical hospitals, it was not widely known what problems I had suffered. I knew there was no way I could consider joining someone's practice without making a clean breast of my situation. I had been invited to consider joining four different surgeons. This of course gave me a real boost. Since I needed to make my situation known anyway I contacted two of the surgeons before being discharged from the hospital. Two who appealed to me were Dr. Bill McDougal, former chief of surgery, and Dr. Charles Robb, to whom I laid out the whole story. He responded by telling me of another young surgeon whom he had personally supported through a bout of depression. He did not seem put off by my problem any more than if I had told him that I was recovering from a severe, prolonged bout of malaria. In the end, I joined Dr. Robb, with whom I worked for the next five years. (I have written about Charles Robb in my essay "My Most Unforgettable Character.")

On August 1, 1963, I began working with Dr. Robb and his group, composed of four others. I became the second surgeon in the group. I had lots of moral support from Charlie Robb. I helped him with his operations, and as I gradually began to get patients of my own he helped me. This was a great arrangement for me, as I began to get my hands back into surgery. But it was by no means easy, as I struggled to regain confidence and started studying for the American Board of Surgery examinations. One of the things I noted, and Dr. B had mentioned, was that depression often begins to lift at about 11 a.m. Others have told me that this does not work for them, but it was very true for me. I would start out the morning depressed and shaky, blindly putting one foot in front of the other, but by the afternoon I would begin to feel much better. In the evening if I was called for an emergency I would often go out feeling that I could lick the world. The uncertainty of the morning was helped by having Charlie available.

While I was taking a medical history a patient told me he had had a nervous breakdown in the past. Not mentioning anything about myself, I asked, "How did you get through it?"

He replied, "I quit my job, went up north in the woods, and built a log cabin."

Curious, I asked, "How long did it take you to recover?"

"Five years," was his answer.

Strangely, that was an encouragement for me. I thought if he could work his way out of it by himself in five years, I could recover faster with skilled help.

One morning at Butterworth Hospital Charlie and I were ready to start an operation, but the intern assigned to our case did not show up. They paged him over and over again, but no show. Finally, somebody started looking for him and found him dead in his car, which was parked in the staff garage. He had hung up an intravenous solution with a known heart-stopping drug and taken his own life. The word came to us before we finished the case. He was a brilliant and promising young doctor. That shook all of us in that operating room, but no one as much as me. By this time I was beginning to desensitize and had made up my mind that this boogeyman was not going to rule me forever. A tragic thing about the intern was that about a week earlier he had told one of the surgeons he wanted to talk to him about something. But the talk never took place. That surgeon was very pained about this. Later, another surgeon, this time a very good friend, also took his life.

I was beginning to learn that a fear could be analyzed, seen to be what it really is, and considered ridiculous. This is what I began to call objectifying it or taking the emotion out of it. Thus I was learning to look my boogeyman in the face and stare him down, so to speak. You don't get anywhere by avoiding disturbing situations. This is one of the principles used in desensitizing people who are afraid of flying.

Another thing I learned during those early months was that certain trigger words or situations would cause me to take an emotional nosedive. I also noticed that it often took me a couple of days before I got back to a good emotional level. So, I reasoned, since I usually work myself back up to a good emotional balance in a couple of days, there must be a way I can jump across that down period more quickly. Figuratively, it was seeing a deep ditch and jumping over it rather than falling into the same pit each time. I did this by recognizing trigger words or situations and then saying to myself unemotionally, "There I go again," and then unemotionally saying to myself, "Nope, not this time"—thus objectively dismissing the fear and refusing to reason with it.

Also, during those early days I talked to Dr. B about occasionally being bombarded by irrational, disturbing thoughts, things too awful to share with anyone. He explained that these are called "compulsive thoughts" and would disappear. He told me of a pastor who had gone through some emotional turbulence. While serving communion, he would sometimes have blasphemous thoughts rushing through his mind. Naturally, this was disturbing beyond imagination. Dr. B had seen him through that successfully. I found that by ignoring the thoughts and minimizing them, they did go away.

Dawn! The Morning Breaks

Early in 1968 and nearing five years in private surgical practice, I contacted Dr. Bergsma about his approval for our return to Africa. I had, of course, been in contact with our mission board as well. Many things had changed, not the least of which were my coping abilities. My vision for Africa had not dimmed. But time moves on with its flow of events—some, mere flotsam but others, never-to-be-forgotten happenings. I had passed both the written and oral American Board of Surgery exams with consequent advancement to a senior surgeon status on two hospital staffs. Before being considered for return, we had to get medical and psychological clearance. This time, both Louise and I took several psychological examinations before Dr. B gave clearance. That was no worry, since I had adequate indication from him that he was ready to let me return to Africa.

Several other major events had transpired. These were the unexpected and premature deaths of Louise's mother and my dad. That made our remaining parents' needs serious considerations to factor in to the equation. Also, the Vietnam conflict was on, and our oldest son, Glenn, who was in his second year of college, had drawn a low number in the Selective Service lottery, meaning he would probably enlist in the military following graduation. The thought of leaving him behind in the U.S. was painful.

In December 1967 my mother and my siblings decided we would all go to Florida for the holidays to avoid Christmas at home, the first one without my dad. Louise and I left for Florida with our boys after my office hours on a Tuesday afternoon. We drove as far as Upland, Indiana, and stayed with my brother Harold. That night Louise handed me the unopened mail, which she had tucked into her suitcase. One was a letter from our mission doctor at Kibogora in Rwanda (originally part of the Burundi mission). The other was from our mission board. The doctor in Rwanda said he would be leaving the coming summer and the hospital needed a replacement. Could I come? The other one was from our mission board. The new director of missions explained that things were different in South Africa (the former doctor was now working for another mission). "Would you please consider returning to South Africa, given the situation has now entirely changed?" he had asked.

It was very amusing, if not laughable. How was I to answer this?

The next day I phoned the director and arranged for an appointment on my way home to Michigan. In Florida, Louise and I discussed the options as we walked the beach together. Frequently, I went alone, asking God to guide us, placing both options in His hands. By the time we were to return I had an answer with which I was totally comfortable.

Reaching mission headquarters at Winona Lake, Louise went to visit her aunt and her dad. I went to meet missions director Charles Kirkpatrick.

"Well, I have an answer for you," I said.

"What is that?" he queried.

"I will go back to South Africa, provided the missionaries in Rwanda and Burundi think that is the place I should go," I said.

Dr. Kirkpatrick threw his head back and began laughing. The subject was dropped.

In August of 1968 we arrived at Kibogora, Rwanda. We had been here many times during our Burundi days when we attended mission meetings or the annual Kumbya Missionary Conference. I became the third mission doctor to serve there since it had been upgraded from a dispensary to a hospital just three years before.

I felt overjoyed to be back in my chosen career. I say chosen because I had the deep conviction that God had chosen this career for me, and I gladly embraced it. Yet I was very aware that I was a wounded healer and had some marks and scars in my psyche from the negative experiences of the previous five years.

I do not hold any grudges against Dr. Rice or the mission board. Lowell Rice was also caught in a very difficult situation. He and I had been pieces in a chess game that neither of us had chosen. We both lost. It resulted in his leaving his beloved Greenville Hospital and going to another church/mission hospital, and for me the bleak experience just described. I anticipate meeting Lowell Rice in heaven, where all tears are wiped away. When we talk we will just laugh. These events will seem like unhappy childhood experiences, now of no consequence. There will be no dark nights of the soul there.

In hindsight, and given my genes, I think the years of depression and psychological pain I had endured were probably inevitable and part of God's plan for me. At least, He had certainly permitted, if not personally designed, them for me.

Back at Kibogora, on a Sunday afternoon I was meditating on the story of Jacob (Gen. 32:22-32) and his early life struggles. On reading about his all-night wrestling with the angel and how he finally admitted his name of Jacob (heel grasper, deceitful one), owning up to what he really was, God changed him and his name. When I read that Jacob went out limping because of his hip, I prayed, "Okay, God, you have permanently wounded me, but I accept it. Here I am. What is left of me and my life, You can have. Just walk with me, that is all I ask."

The following is excerpted from my book, *On a Hill Far Away*. There is some repetition, but I am leaving it that way to reinforce the points and lessons that I learned from my "dark night of the soul" experience.

Depression is something I have had to battle, in various degrees, most of my life. In my early years I didn't recognize it. I just supposed everyone had the same kinds of ups and downs. My first real episode that I could not shake without help hit me in 1963 when I was thirty-six years old. We had gone to South Africa at the request of our mission board. We were sent into a situation full of conflict to replace a doctor who refused to be replaced. Without going into details, I would simply say, I broke under it and pulled out, returning to the U.S.A. I felt tremendous guilt, worthlessness, and hopelessness. Thoughts of suicide would dog me—not that I seriously considered it as an option, but the fact I even thought of it filled my heart with terror. I could not sleep except for short periods. When I did sleep, I would always awaken around 3:30 or 4 a.m. My mind would seize upon a problem, a past sin, or supposed sin. My emotions and thought would go into a spasm, like a cramp in the muscle of a leg. Sometimes, an unwitting remark from a friend, even something from a sermon, would throw me into despair. Reading the newspaper was impossibly upsetting. Even Scripture could ignite my fears and darken my thoughts. I had to confine myself to an encouraging psalm—usually the thirty-fourth. I lost my appetite and began to lose weight. My mouth would be dry all the time. I was always tired but rarely sleepy.

My condition was beyond my control and I saw that I needed outside help. I turned to Dr. David Stewart, a psychiatrist friend, whom I had known in Burundi. He recognized my condition immediately as an anxiety-depressive reaction and insisted I get treatment. Dr. Stuart Bergsma, another former missionary turned psychiatrist, from my hometown of Grand Rapids, Michigan, became my doctor.

I was out of commission for four or five months before I practiced medicine again. I owe my recovery to God of course, but three people helped me very much. The first was my wife, Louise, with her steady, uncritical support and ready listening ear. The second was Dr. Bergsma, with his counseling and medications. The third was Dr. Charlie Robb, who took me into the practice of surgery with him. He even, eventually, had me operate on him! These people believed in me when I didn't believe in myself. They were sure I would get better, and I did.

I don't believe anyone should ever consider oneself completely cured from depression. Just as those in Alcoholics Anonymous call themselves recovering alcoholics, we need to recognize our propensity to depression and constantly be on guard to keep the upper hand. In 1991 with the change back from foreign missionary service to U.S. medical practice, plus facing retirement, I felt myself in a spiral downward toward another depression. This time I knew what was happening and went for help early. It turned out to be a minor episode, and I did get through it with the help of a Christian psychiatrist and managed to work full-time throughout those dark days.

In early 1993, thirty years after my original major depression of 1963, but just pulling out of this minor relapse, we packed up and went back to Africa to face the events recorded in my book *On a Hill Far Away: Journal of a Missionary Doctor in Rwanda*. Thus my struggles emotionally are evident in the entries. Also, my whole missionary career has been a type of quest for the Holy Grail, that is, a pursuit of God and an effort to know Him, to believe Him, to serve Him. I hope that this quest is also evident in the entries.

Because of these "dark night of the soul" experiences, which I passed through, I have been able to help others. These are some of the things I have learned:

1. Depression can hit anyone, anytime (but in my opinion most often in mid-life). J.B. Phillips, Bible translator of *Letters to Young Churches* and other books, experienced a recurring and at times disabling depression. His wife, with the help of Edwin Robertson, wrote about this in *J.B. Phillips, the Wounded Healer*. Phillips himself wrote about it in *The Price of Success*: "I can only testify to the fact that it would have been of inestimable comfort and encouragement to me in some of my darkest hours if I could have come across even one book written by someone who had experienced and survived the hellish torments of mind which can be produced...This chapter must be written by someone who has experienced the almost unendurable sense of terror and alienation."

2. It is helpful to know that you will get better. If I can just hang on, depression eventually passes like hay fever at the end of the ragweed season. It may be weeks, months, or years (usually months), but it does go away.

3. Seek professional help if depression persists for weeks or becomes intolerable, and don't be afraid to use prescribed medicines.

4. Depression often lifts in the afternoon. I used to think that if I could just get through to 11 a.m., things would be okay. Learn to objectify it and look upon it as an inconvenience, like a bad headache.

5. Keep busy and occupied even when you don't feel like it. E. Stanley Jones said, "You can act your way into right thinking easier than you can think your way into right acting."

6. Find a sympathetic ear (mine was my wife's), but don't unload on multiple ears.

7. I used cognitive therapy on myself. This is described by David D. Burns, M.D. in *Feeling Good: The New Mood Therapy* and *The Feeling Good Handbook*. Also, along the same lines but from an evangelical viewpoint is *Learning to Tell Yourself the Truth* by William Backus and Marie Chapian.

8. I could function even when I was scared and miserable. Keep going. Alcoholics Anonymous has this expression: "Fake it to make it."

9. It is unwise to make major changes in employment, resi-
dence, marital status, and so forth, when going through
emotional turmoil. (I admit I violated this rule somewhat in
going back to Africa, but in a sense I was going home.)
10. Don't confuse emotional turmoil with spiritual turmoil.
When depression comes in, faith often goes out. Doggedly
I hung on like Job, saying, "Though He slay me, yet will I
trust Him."[1]

Finally, one of the most important lessons I have learned from my
experience is to live completely outside my introspective mentality.
For me, I am happiest when I am unaware of my inner feelings and
looking outward.

It is like the room temperature. I am most comfortable when I am
unaware of the temperature. That is to say, I am not aware that the
temperature is too hot or too cold. The temperature is just right when
I am not aware that there is such a thing as temperature. Similarly, I
am at peace when I am not aware of happiness, sadness, anxiety, or
other inner emotions—totally unaware of my inner self.

Charlie, My Most Unforgettable Character

He was a giant in my eyes, even though he was much shorter than I. He was twelve years older—not really like a father figure, maybe like an older brother. His name was Dr. Charles Stuart Robb, one of the Grand Rapids surgeons at Butterworth Hospital, where I had gone to intern in 1953. He was one of those rare people whom you always are happy to see, someone who always seems interested in you.

I guess my first memories of him were when I would be invited, along with several other interns or residents and our wives, to his house for supper. Here we met his wife, Lynette, a nurse he had married while he was an intern in Detroit. I could not have imagined that one day we would be in practice together at 445 Cherry Street. Nor could I ever have foreseen that someday, he and Lynette would come all the way to Africa to visit us. There, they made themselves at home working with us. We traveled through the mountains, circling the lakes of Rwanda and Uganda; we drove a Land Rover through game parks together, dodging elephants at night as we tried to locate a safari lodge. We fished on the Nile. Charlie and Lynette relished it and said it was the best vacation they had ever taken.

For the next thirty years our contacts were only by letter, a brief visit to his house on our way through Grand Rapids, or occasionally sharing a meal together. But it did not matter; just a telephone call, a brief visit, a letter—things were always the same. Charlie and I would pick up right where we left off.

One day in April of 1998 the phone rang at our cottage.

"Al, this is Keith Robb." It could only be bad news. Keith never phoned me.

He came immediately to the reason for his call. "Charlie passed away yesterday, Easter Sunday. There was a fire around his house in the country; it was getting near his neighbor's house as well as his own. He had been battling to contain it before the fire department arrived. They found him sitting against a tree, his rake at hand, dead."

I was not surprised to learn that there would be no public funeral, just a simple family service. Charlie had always told me he did not want any fuss when he went. "They can just roll me over in the gutter if they want," he said.

My time of close contact with Dr. Robb totaled ten years, five years in training with him as one of my surgery mentors, then five years as a partner, and the rest as a friend. He is gone now, but people like that never leave. In a way their spirit is always with you. It is like my father or mother; I know what they, or Charlie, would say to almost any question or problem that arises. I sort of have them near by, cheering me on, or telling me what I should do next, or sometimes making me feel ashamed, as I realize that they would not have said this or done that.

I quote Charlie so often that I think our sons are now using the quotes. They were crisp, to the point, always containing a lesson and representing lots of thought. One of Charlie's sayings was, "God hates a coward." I was not sure that was really in the Bible, but it does say "Fear not" in a lot of places. What Charlie meant was, "Don't be scared to do something. If you've got to do it, do it!" He often would tell me, "It is like climbing a ladder; you can't stay halfway up just shaking—you might as well get going, and get to the top and do what you have to do." He admitted that heights used to scare him, but as with every other fear he would not permit it to conquer him.

Another thing he used to say, and of all places in surgery, was this: "Don't just stand there; get in trouble." Then he would throw his head back and guffaw. That was his version of "Don't just stand there, do something." Or if I asked his opinion as to when I should do something, he would always say, "There's no time like the present." Those words still come to me, especially if I'm tempted to procrastinate about something or make an excuse to not do the hard thing now. Putting something off can be ruinous. My father's version of the same thing was a quote from some sage who said, "Procrastination is the thief of time."

Sometimes we would be making rounds together, and Charlie would say, "Let's drop in and say hello to Mrs. Jones."

I would ask, "Why, is she a patient of our office?"

He would reply, "No, but I know her. Keep your lines open." He was always going out of his way to help someone, and it was not out of selfishness, as those words might imply. He just never wrote anyone off. One time an old general practitioner who had had a stroke was in the hospital, comatose. Charlie says to me, "Let's stop in and see old Ballard."

I never particularly liked Ballard and did not at all respect him as a doctor. I wondered, "Why should we go in to see old Ballard?"

Selfishly, I thought, "What did he ever do for me, or how will he even know we stopped in?" But Charlie thought differently. Here was an old colleague who was dying, and even if he could not respond, Charlie was going to stop in, give him a couple of affectionate pats, and say, "Ballard, old horse, how are you doing?" Charlie believed in doing to others as he would like others to do to him.

Before I ever thought of practicing with him, I wrote Charlie a letter from the ship on which we were sailing to Africa. I expressed my great appreciation for all he had taught me and how he had helped me with my philosophy of practicing medicine, and I thanked him for being such a great friend. I was not thinking of keeping my lines open at that time, but as it turned out that is just what I was doing. When the assignment I was going to in South Africa did not pan out, we found ourselves back in Grand Rapids sooner than expected. Four surgeons indicated that I could have a place with them, but the invitation I felt the best about was the one to work with Charlie and his group of three internists and a family practitioner.

The Cherry Street group was worried because Charlie had had a transient ischemic episode, or a TIA, as it is called. He had gone through a series of neurological studies, and it was learned that his carotid arteries were blocked on both sides. He also had hypertension and had suffered from nephritis since childhood. He never thought he would live long, and he had long since quit worrying about it. But his colleagues had asked him to lighten up, get a younger surgeon to work with him, and take it easier. It was a dream come true for me, since I would immediately get into lots of surgery, gain experience, and work with someone I really respected. Referring to his own condition, Charlie said to me about his carotid arteries and his brain, "Well, we don't know how the blood gets up there, but the studies show it gets up there some way, probably through the vertebral and basilar arteries." So he was on blood thinners and trying to slow down.

I will never forget an incident in those early days. Charlie learned that I had taken a membership out at the health club at the YMCA and was playing paddleball there during the noon hour. So Charlie decided he would like to do the same. Several times a week we would meet at the Y, play paddleball or handball, take a quick swim, and be done in time to get to office by 2 p.m. One day I slammed a hard one, and the ball hit him right in the back of the head. I was horrified and apologetic, but he just groaned and laughed it off. But another time he went back to the wall to make a shot, lost his balance, and slammed his head against the wall. He sank to the floor, his head in his hands, and moaned. I hovered over him wondering if I should call an ambulance. I watched him closely, afraid he would lose consciousness. I feared that being on blood thinners, he could be hemorrhaging inside the head. I also noted that his scalp was bleeding through his hair.

He began to look around, stirred, then got up, and said, "Okay, let's play."

I said, "You gotta be kidding! Let's go to the office."

He insisted, "No, I'm all right. Let's finish the game."

After the game and in the locker room, a fellow looked at him and said, "Hey, your head is bleeding. You better gets some clips or stitches in that."

I replied, "Yeah, we're both in that racket; we're going to the office now to do it." So that is what we did; we went to the office, set up some instruments, and I sewed up Charlie's scalp.

When I first met Charlie, he cursed freely when it fit the occasion, but as time went by, we had many deep and interesting philosophical discussions. These often were on religious subjects. Little by little, I noticed that Charlie no longer was swearing; in fact he had started to attend the Christian Medical Society Saturday morning Bible studies with me. His thirst for things spiritual became very noticeable. He had come across a book, *Beyond Ourselves* by Catherine Marshall, that someone had given to his wife. He had started to read it and could hardly put it down.

Charlie needed an operation for hernia repair. He asked me to be his surgeon. I was flattered but scared because of his medical history of other, more serious conditions. One of our internal medicine partners was worried also. In fact, he had made Lynette very uncomfortable, saying, "Don't worry, Lynette. If something happens to Charlie, our group will take care of you." He meant she would have no financial worries. This really worried Lynette, and I began to chicken out. So one evening I phoned Charlie at home to talk him out of the operation. But no way.

Charlie simply said to me, "Al, when you say your prayers tonight, just tell God, 'I'm only going to put his anatomy back the way it is supposed to be. Whether he lives or not is up to You.'"

That remark was reminiscent of something he had told me long before, when I was in training: "We are not responsible for everything that happens. The outcome of an operation depends on three things: you as the surgeon, the patient's ability to heal and fight disease, and God."

The night before he was to have the operation, we were both in the office late. I stopped by his office on my way out. Charlie was obviously thinking very seriously. He knew I had had some pretty serious illnesses myself, and he knew about the experience I had gone through with severe depression.

This evening as I stepped into his office he asked, "Al, how did you pray when you were sick?" I told him I did not pray primarily for my healing, but I prayed that God would take over my life. I told him of an experience as a teenager, when I felt so inadequate to change myself that I had prayed for deliverance from my sins and for His strength. I told him how I had reached my hand up to heaven and felt as though God had taken hold of my hand and said, "I will be your strength." And I told him how real that had been. I also told him about a time that a verse of Scripture, Romans 5:1, had jumped off the page and hit home to me. The Scripture was, "Therefore, being justified by faith we have peace with God, through our Lord Jesus Christ." I told him some of the sins I was addicted to. I told him that even though I had been reared in a very religious home and was the grandson of a preacher, I had to come to know God for myself.

Immediately, Charlie brightened up and said, "That is just what Catherine (Marshall) said: 'God has no grandchildren.'"

As I left he said, "Al, you just witnessed to me."

The next day we did the surgery. I had another colleague help me for moral support. Things went well. The day after surgery, I came in to see him, and after doing my medical checks, I said to him, "You know, I was thinking about what you said, about God having no grandchildren, and I thought of a Scripture for you."

He eagerly asked, "What is it?'

I said, "It is John 1:12," which reads, "But as many as received Him, to them He gave the right to become children of God, to those who believe in His name."

He pulled the Gideon Bible from his bedside stand and read it out loud several times. Then he closed the Bible and said, "So be it!"

For me, and I think for Charlie, that was his confession of faith. He had been journeying toward God for a long time. He now was a son of God. From then on we had Christian fellowship as Christian brothers. I never doubted his relationship with God, and I don't believe he did either.

As several more years passed, I grew to admire this guy more and more. He just did not seem to care what anyone thought. He was well off financially, but he never wasted a penny. One time he took off his suit jacket and threw it on a chair as he put on a hospital gown to go into an isolation room. I noticed the label inside; it read, "Robert Hall," one of the cheapest places you could find clothes. Charlie, being short, had a hard time finding clothes that were not too large for him. Another time I saw a coat thrown over a chair; I noted that the label read, "Boys Department." What did it matter to him as long as it fit? Who cared what anyone thought? I was amused, and it did not worry me either, because to me he was a giant.

We were making rounds one day when we met Dr. J, a gynecologist. Dr. J. was looking over the charts at the nursing station and found one of his former patients under Charlie's name. Snooping through the chart, he learned that Charlie had done an appendectomy.

He held the chart in his hand, accosting Charlie with, "Don't you know I do appendectomies?"

"Yeah, I know you do appendectomies," Charlie replied, and walked on.

He said to me, "I felt like saying, 'Yeah, I know you do appendectomies, but when the patient tells me they want me to do it rather than you, then I do it.'"

"Why didn't you tell him that?" I asked.

"I didn't want to hurt him," he replied.

Occasionally, the reverse happened. I would notice that one of our supposedly loyal patients was in the hospital under someone else's care. If I mentioned this to Charlie, it never upset him; he would quickly ask, "Well, did she get the right treatment?"

There again, with one question, he would cut through all the nonsense of ego or turf protection and dramatize to me the purpose of practicing medicine: curing people.

Sometimes, I would make negative statements about someone, which seemed so obvious that I supposed it to be true. Charlie, always ready to give another person the benefit of the doubt, would simply reply, "We don't know that!" That has helped me so many times through the years, when my wife and I would be wondering about a perceived slight, something someone said, or what they meant or did or didn't do. When we are tempted to jump to a conclusion, I quote Charlie and say, "We don't know that." Those words are a good antidote to the bad habit of mind-reading.

Charlie never said anything bad about anyone. About the worst thing he would ever say was, "It takes all kinds to make a world." Or he might say, "Well, there's room in the world for him." I do, however, remember one funny story and some unflattering remarks by Charlie. There was an old, flamboyant, Southern gentleman surgeon whom most of us in training had a lot of fun imitating. It seems that when Charlie was in training, Dr. JCF, who did many things on the spur of the moment, asked Charlie to bring a couple of other young doctors and their wives to his farm for supper. At the appointed hour, Charlie and Lynette, with two other couples, showed up at the farm all dressed for dinner. Mrs. JCF invited them in, explaining that JC had not come home from the office as yet. After about an hour of small talk, "Shug" (short for Sugar, as JC called her) asked, "Did JC, perchance, invite you folks to dinner?" Charlie was horrified and terribly embarrassed, trying to slip out as gracefully as possible, but "Shug" would not hear to it. She and her servant went into action and prepared a banquet of Southern fried chicken. Dr. JCF, by then home, presided over the grand affair as if nothing out of the normal had taken place.

I suppose you judge a person by how they treat you, and Dr. JCF had always treated me wonderfully, buying me surgical instruments to take to Africa or sending some to me from time to time. So, one day as Charlie and I were scrubbing up for an operation in the room where JCF usually operated, we were commenting on the old guy and his idiosyncrasies.

I said, "Well, it will be a sad day when he is gone."

Charlie replied, "Yes, but there won't be many tears shed!" Then he quickly added, "And my eyes will be driest of all."

As those remarks show, Charlie was very good with words and could always say things in a different way from other people. It was only after being around him for a long time that I realized he must have had a tendency to stutter in his early years. I could sometimes see his lips moving before emitting a sound. I never wanted to ask him about it. I just figured it must represent one more thing he had overcome in his life.

His wisdom and ability to see through all the fluff and tinsel in our society was dramatized on another occasion that I remember very clearly. We were operating at Butterworth Hospital. We were in Room One, across the hall from the doctors' lounge. Surgery has its moments of high drama, but it also has its times of tedium, like when the abdomen is being closed. At these times there often is a lot of banter; it's a time when the nurses get to chattering about this and that. Charlie was busy working, with his head in the wound as always, since he was nearsighted. One of the circulating nurses entered the room all excited, saying that Dr. T., one of the surgery residents, had just gotten engaged to one of the senior student nurses. That provoked much excitement; they gushed about how beautiful this girl was, a veritable Miss America.

Charlie, from behind his mask, head down, working hard, and sick of all the emphasis on her physical attributes, asks, "Yes, but is she nice?"

The prattle continued with no answer to Charlie, so he repeated, "Yes, but is she nice?" The conversation went on, and Charlie was still being ignored, as though he was talking to the stomach.

He and I were very fond of Dr. T., so Charlie raised his head, turned, and shouted, "Yes, but is she nice?"

Once again Charlie had zeroed in on the most important thing. Lynette, his wife, was both beautiful and nice, and he knew that being nice held marriages together a lot better than being beautiful did. For me I picked up one more quote that helped me to see the most important thing. I apply that question to a lot of things, often summing up a discussion at home with, "Yes, but is she nice?"

Charlie's optimism was contagious. In his early days of practice, a lady who needed an operation came to him. When he suggested surgery, she looked at him, thought he looked awfully young and boyish, and doubted she wanted to go along with him as surgeon. Charlie related, "I said to her, 'Mrs. Smith, I'm not very smart, but I am awfully lucky.' When I told her that, she decided to have me do it." Then he threw his head back, roaring with laughter.

I mentioned to Lynette one time how he seemed to never worry and just loved surgery. She said, "That's right. Once he had to do a cholecystectomy on my sister. I thought he would be worried, but that morning when he left the house, he just bounded out the door, like a happy young school boy."

He never took hard situations or good or bad results personally. I remember getting on the elevator with a little child being taken to surgery and crying his heart out. As we left the elevator I said to Charlie, "It kind of breaks your heart, doesn't it?" He replied, "Yes, but you've got to know, we're trying to help him." Lesson: things seen in their right perspective are less painful.

Was Charlie really "awfully lucky," as he told Mrs. Smith? I always thought it was just his optimistic outlook on life. Maybe he just thought he was lucky. I had a chance to put this to an objective test. At the time he and Lynette came to Africa, the last adventure we had together was a fishing expedition on the Nile. Charlie and I, with my sons Steve and Dan, drove out from Kampala in Uganda to the Nile River; here it flows north from Lake Victoria. It was a very remote area, where not many tourists or white people go. We rented a small boat with an outboard motor and an African to operate it while we trolled up and down the river. It is not unusual to pull in large Nile perch of thirty to fifty pounds. Fish seem to know that I am not a real fisherman. My sons and I had fished here before; no fish thought it worth their trouble to go after my line. The day Charlie went along, it was different. They seemed to sense that a lucky fisherman was holding one of the poles. An optimist exudes some mystical powers that pull fish to the hook. So, of course, Charlie had several strikes and each time pulled in a Nile perch. We went home with two beauties, nine pounds each. These were relatively small by local standards but still were whoppers for someone from Michigan. Back at the guesthouse Charlie and the boys filleted them. What a luscious dinner we had that evening.

I also learned from Charlie how important it is to express appreciation. During the years we practiced surgery together, he would often get a cards of appreciation from our patients. I would often find such a card on my desk. I once picked one up and looked at it curiously. I was more curious about why Charlie had put the card on my desk than about the card itself. It seemed like such a little, inconsequential thing. I guess I figured that if you wanted to express appreciation, you needed to send a gift, like a box of candy or nuts, or something bought on a trip. I read the card and took it back to Charlie with a comment like, "That was nice of her, wasn't it?" Charlie just beamed as he laid the card back on his desk. Later, as I began to receive little tokens of appreciation, I experienced the joy a doctor feels from simple things like cards. Patients don't know how much a doctor carries their burdens, prays about operations, or tosses and turns the night before a big case. Just a little expression of appreciation becomes a great reward. I have ever since tried to show in some way how much we appreciate the doctors who have helped us.

Another thing about Charlie that really dumbfounded me: when a patient died, he would call at the funeral home, pay his respects and sign the book, speak his condolences to the family, and leave. I remember one case very clearly. Everything went wrong, and the poor man seemed to have one complication after another until finally he died. For me, I felt like leaving town, hiding from the lawyers, and staying as far away as I could, but not Charlie. He went to the funeral home, talked with the family, showed his great sympathy, and left. From his standpoint, why wouldn't he do that? After all, as he had told me once before, "You've got to know, we're trying to help them." And Mr. D. was "one of our people," as he called our patients.

Charlie never expected to live to a ripe old age. He had suffered from chronic nephritis since childhood. This resulted in hypertension as an adult. Then, as mentioned earlier, right in the prime of life, he had a TIA, a result of blocked carotid arteries. None of these things ever slowed him down. Perhaps that is why he seemed to treat each day as a gift and live it as though it were his last. He had told Lynette early on that he did not expect to live long. During the day when he would get a phone call from her, he would talk with so much excitement, laughing and bantering back and forth, that you felt as if he was talking to his girlfriend.

A couple of years before he died, on one of our trips home from Africa, I phoned him for our usual updating, and he told me that he had had a slight heart attack in early December. I asked for details.

"Well, I felt this pain in my chest on Friday, so I just took it easy and laid around. Saturday, it was still more or less there. Finally, I decided that I would go in and check it out on Monday."

"Monday? Why didn't you go in Friday night or Saturday?"

"Oh, they wouldn't have done anything on the weekend!"

"Charlie, you could have died on the weekend!"

"Yeah, maybe," he said. Then he began to laugh as he told me that his kids had gotten him skis for Christmas. I just shook my head in amazement.

The day I got the call from his youngest son, Keith, telling me Charlie had passed on, I suppose I could have said, "Well, Charlie's luck finally ran out." But instead, I wrote to the family expressing my sympathy and my great sense of loss, but I added: "If you could have given Charlie the option of how he would choose to die, like from an accident, an illness, or dwindling down and falling asleep, which one would he have chosen?" I went on, "I can just see him: the grass fire getting out of hand; his thinking to himself, 'That wind is really whipping this up, but I'll get it under control, I can handle this.' Fighting, fighting, fighting, until he had to sit down, lean against a tree to get a few breaths, and let the chest pain subside."

I got a letter back from his oldest son, Bill, saying, "At first, I was thinking that maybe Charlie had been a bit unwise that day, but after reading your letter, I would have to agree—the way he died was exactly how he would have chosen to go."

For me, that represented my friend Charlie: unpretentious, brilliant, humble, intuitive, honest, the best friend I could ever hope to have. I can visualize him, after eighty-four years of living life to the fullest, standing unafraid at the pearly gates. When St. Peter asks him why he thought he should be let in, he would reply, "Well, Pete, I've never been real smart, but I'm awfully lucky."

Then St. Peter would reply, "Yes, Charlie, you are awfully lucky, but lucky because Christ died for your sins, and you accepted that fact a long time ago. Welcome. Come right in!"

Charlie probably threw his head back and guffawed, answering, "So be it!"

Louise—My True Love

I thought true love would never hit me. I had finished high school and was at the advanced age of seventeen; every love I had experienced, from grade school up, had faded away.

My older brother had been swept off his feet early in high school. My mother worried about my being attracted to one of the Dutch girls who were so numerous in the Grand Rapids area. She said when a boy marries a Dutch girl they all end up as members of the Christian Reformed Church. It was like the movie where the Greek father keeps complaining and lamenting, "But he's not Greek! He's not Greek!" Only, with Mom, it was, "She's not of our church. She's not of our church."

When I went into the army I started writing to Mary, a girl from our church. She was in our youth group. We had never really dated, but lonesome soldiers have a need to feel serious, so in our letters a love affair by mail began. Overseas, in the Philippine Islands, lonely and far away from home, mail call was the bright spot of the week.

After a time, I began to locate other Free Methodist friends stationed in the same area. Chet, a boyhood friend from my home church, had enlisted in the Merchant Marines. That eventually brought him to the Far East. Whenever his ship docked in Manila, he would spend a few days with me. He was corresponding with Ruth, another girl from our home church. When we were together we shared each other's letters and dreamed of the day we would be back home.

On the other side of the world at a summer camp in New Jersey, two Greenville College students were working as counselors. One was Ruth, Chet's pen pal love, and the other, from Indiana, was Louise Vore. Ruth showed Louise a photo of Chet and me in Manila. She told her all about Chet and his friend Al Snyder, explaining, "Al's family and my family are friends. He will be coming to Greenville College when he gets out of the army." She insisted, "I know Al, and you are just the kind of girl he will marry."

The war ended, and months later I ended up at Greenville College. Through various and strange ways that only God and Cupid understand, Chet ended up dating and eventually marrying (my) Mary, not Ruth.

The college had planned some special activities for those students remaining on campus over the long Thanksgiving weekend. Curiously, I ended up with a group of students on a scavenger hunt. As we went from place to place, I began to get acquainted with some of the girls in the party. As we were walking along, one engaged me in conversation, asking me many questions. As I responded, I learned that she was a senior and her father was a doctor in East Chicago. We discovered many coincidences. I did not know that this girl, Louise Vore, had gotten the lowdown on me from Ruth at camp the previous summer. But as the web began to spin around me, I was fascinated and intrigued. So artfully did she proceed that I did not think it strange that this senior student knew so much about me. She asked me questions and I replied, discovering many interesting parallels between her life and mine. I say, "I discovered," but they were things she already knew and was helping me to learn for myself. Her father and mother had gone to Greenville College with my father and mother; her dad had gone to medical school in Ann Arbor with my dad.

I went back to my dorm that night determined to check out this Louise Vore further. But I did not know that she went back to her dorm thinking, "Well, I have finally met the guy Ruth said, 'You are just the kind of girl Al will marry.'"

A few more dates, and I was a captive. Love, which I had heard so much about, hit me with an intensity I did not think possible. My brother was already at Greenville. His wife, whom I had known from high school days, taunted me with, "Al, it won't last. Louise Vore has gone with a lot of great guys, and she throws them over every time. I'll give you two weeks."

That served as a stimulus to me. I replied, "It won't be the case this time."

I began meeting Louise in the evening, having dinner together at the college cafeteria. When I arrived at Burritt Hall to meet her for supper she would be waiting, playing a classic piece on the piano the quality of which I had never heard before. I learned she was the practice accompanist for the A Cappella Choir and accompanist for the voice students. After dinner we would take a walk and play Ping-Pong or tennis. She could beat me at both. What kind of girl was this? Her brown eyes and brown hair were the most beautiful I had ever seen. I even loved her pug nose, probably because all Snyders had aquiline noses. My mother's family had passed blue eyes down to my siblings, and my mother always tried to believe I had brown eyes, even though they were a disappointing hazel. The big brown eyes of this girl melted me.

Never did I get the impression that she was being swept off her feet by me. As we separated for the Christmas holidays, I gave her a rather expensive pen and pencil set for Christmas; she gave me a wrapped present to open on Christmas Day. When I opened her present at our family Christmas, I found a modest box of men's soap. Even this struck me as a perfect gift.

My younger brother taunted me with, "She is trying to tell you to take a bath."

My mother lamented, "With all the nice things you got from your family, you just sit there mooning over those three bars of soap."

But she did not know that the fragrance and intimacy of that soap cast a spell over me that was not explainable. After all, where does one use bath soap? The fragrance of that soap portended exciting visions for the future.

Back at college, after the holidays, I had my mind made up. This was the "one and only" I had always hoped would come into my life. I presumed she was feeling the same way. One evening she grasped my hand and exclaimed, "Oh, I like you."

I responded with, "I know it. You love me."

That was a king-size blunder. The rest of the evening she froze. I did not know why. I kissed her goodnight, and it was like kissing the refrigerator door. I pondered it overnight and decided to talk it out the next day. I had no idea what had gone wrong, but with a little discussion I learned that she would be the one to tell me when she loved me, and I did not need to make such assumptions unless I heard it from her. Apparently, she was not yet ready to give me that assurance. Oh dear, would I ever understand women?

But the day did come when she told me she loved me, although this was long after I had been telling her how much I was in love with her.

Louise graduated from Greenville, and we separated for summer vacation. We exchanged letters, and she visited my house in June to attend my sister's wedding. Somehow, we both knew we would be next as things were moving inexorably along that path. I can't remember any formal proposal; we just discussed marriage until we were finally ready to announce a date. The only thing I made abundantly clear was that in the Philippine Islands I had felt a call to foreign missions. So the question had several parts: would she marry me, and would she go overseas with me as a missionary? And what if I did not get into medical school, or become a doctor like her dad and my dad? The answer was not only that she would marry me, but also she would go with me wherever God wanted me to go, and she would marry me even if I became a garbage man. In those days, in the Free Methodist church, a nice watch substituted for an engagement ring. That made things cheaper for me. I wrote her father for permission, and we were married in La Due Chapel at Greenville College just before Christmas vacation 1947.

Louise had signed an eighteen-hundred dollar contract to teach sixth grade in Alton, Illinois. Not much money to live on, but acceptable for those days. Each day she traveled forty-five miles to Alton. She shared expenses with three other girls. Unfortunately, Christmas vacation started on Friday afternoon at Greenville, but Alton schools were to continue on Monday and Tuesday of the Christmas week. That made our honeymoon start in St. Louis the first night with a delay en route for Louise to teach two more days in Alton before starting our trip down south. I had saved some money for this, and the day of the wedding my father gave me an additional two hundred dollars, so we felt rich as we headed south in a borrowed 1947 Chevrolet, kindness of my brother Art. We had no particular destination in mind other than thinking it would be nice to see the Gulf of Mexico. We were both twenty-one and felt able to take on the world. I don't think we even knew what medical insurance was, but I'm sure at least that the car was insured. Since I had kept my army life insurance, I was worth ten thousand dollars dead, but not much alive. Oh, the bliss of youth!

We had followed a road map to reach New Orleans, arriving sometime in late afternoon on Christmas Day. Obviously, I had not studied the geography of the area, because each time I asked directions on how to get to the gulf, people would look at me blankly and shake their heads. Finally, we found a road going out of town in a southwest direction. We followed this for about an hour when it turned into a dirt road going through sugarcane fields on each side. As it began to get dark we came to a small village and found a small white frame hotel. We pulled up to the curb. A noisy bar, with blaring music, was located next door. We walked into a small vestibule of the hotel and asked if they had a room. The lady at the desk gave us a quizzical look that seemed to say, "Do you kids really know what you are asking?" There we stood, two twenty-one year-olds, without wedding rings, at eight o'clock in the evening, looking so bewildered and innocent that the good lady finally said, "We will arrange it, but be sure to keep your door locked. There is a lot of drinking going on tonight."

We carried our bags up to a small room where things looked and smelled strangely like the oil-drilling rigs so prevalent in the area. I turned one of the pillows over, and it was black from the greasy head that had used it last.

Louise said, "Let's not stay here."

"But we have already paid," I replied.

"Just ask for it back," she insisted.

Here I gave in to my bride and said, "If you can get our money back, we can drive back to New Orleans."

She rose to the occasion, and with our money we left.

59

As we were putting our things back into the car, a rough character, full of "Christmas cheer," came out of the bar, climbed on his motorcycle, revved up the engine, and with a roar took off. The next thing we saw was the man lying on the ground, his motorcycle still roaring as it spun out of control, driverless, in a semicircle, crashing not far from us. We hastily climbed into our car and headed back up the dirt road toward New Orleans, arriving around midnight. We checked into a respectable motel. Thus ended our first Christmas as Mr. and Mrs. Al Snyder.

The miracle of all this is that Louise continued to follow me into a future that would take us to many more exotic places and exciting situations than that first Christmas together somewhere in the Mississippi Delta.

The following day our honeymoon adventures began to improve as we traveled east along the Gulf of Mexico. We went as far as Biloxi, Mississippi, now an area filled with casinos, but in 1947 a quiet town on a beautiful beach. Mid-afternoon, we checked into a nice hotel. My bride was reassured about being married to a young guy who did not have a clue where he was going. She thought life with me might not be so bad after all. We explored the beach area, rented a small boat to row around a quiet lagoon, and went out to a pleasant tiny island.

Another memorable event surfaced at this stop. As we unloaded the car completely for the first time, I could not find a new blue suit, my going-away garb the night we fled the wedding reception. It was not exactly new, but I had been saving it for a few months, knowing that my father would no longer be buying my clothes. And not only that, it had cost $65, which was very expensive for those days. I phoned back to the hotel in St. Louis, and of course no one had seen it. My dejection was so marked that Louise wondered if I regretted having gotten married. I knew I had worn it into the hotel the night of our wedding but could not remember seeing it after that. Eventually I threw off that disaster and was comforted in knowing that I still had an old brown suit back at Greenville. Anyway, who cares about clothes on their honeymoon?

We continued on through Mobile and Pensacola, visiting the beautiful Belangrath gardens with their gorgeous display of azaleas and camellias. The gardener took a shine to Louise and picked her a beautiful camellia to wear in her hair. We drove up through southern Alabama to the town of Opp and hunted up an old army buddy, Ewen Moody. Moody was an only child and still lived with his parents on a small farm in an unpainted gray clapboard house. It was built on log stumps, without central heating or any of the niceties of our northern homes. His family delighted in serving us some lukewarm cane juice, which Louise almost gagged on. (In later years, Moody became a pharmacist, married, and established Moody's Drugs in Florala, Alabama).

Our honeymoon was almost over. That night we stayed in a motel in Huntsville, Alabama. The next day, running out of time and money, we drove more than six hundred miles to Louise's home in East Chicago, Indiana.

Back in Greenville we moved into the upstairs apartment of a duplex. Louise resumed her teaching and the daily drives to Alton, and I went back to my college studies. About three months later Louise began to suffer from nausea. Our Glenn was born six months after that, a little over eleven months after our wedding. Louise had gone home for the delivery, and I was temporarily alone in Greenville.

After I brought Louise and the baby back to Greenville, one of our friends was baby-sitting for the children of the academic dean, who lived on the other side of an adjoining wall. This friend later told us that our baby's crying could be heard inside the dean's duplex, and the five-year-old son said to her, "That is the Snyders' baby crying. They have only been married eleven months. Do you think that is long enough?" That let us know that we had been the subject of discussions at some of the faculty wives' parties.

Over the next nine years Louise presented me with three more sons, making four children. Their birthdates have always been easy for me to remember. Glenn was born while I was in college; Bob while I as in medical school; Steve while I was in surgical residency; and Dan while I was studying tropical medicine in Belgium. Happily, we never had two in diapers at the same time. Eventually, we began to expect only sons and not daughters. After our third one, when Louise was told it was another boy, she said to me, "Oh no, now I have three to mop up after in the bathroom." Later, when our fourth son, Dan, was born in Belgium, we dubbed him our Brussels sprout. Louise looks back and laments that we did not have six kids.

Now, after more than fifty years of marriage to Louise, and having lived on three continents, producing four children, eight grandchildren, and three great grandchildren. I can affirm, "...now abide faith, hope, love, these three; but the greatest of these is love" (1 Cor. 13:13).

Part Two:

Observations along the Way

Built-in Forgiveness

To ask forgiveness is to admit you did something wrong. It is not fun. It never has been one of my favorite things. Some people would rather do something nice for you than to verbalize an apology—like my dad, who never did like asking forgiveness. His method was to send a check. I learned that was his way of saying "I'm sorry." It was a pretty good deal for me. My children might have preferred Dad's way—the check, I mean.

There's a family story about Dad when he was nine years old and fighting with his older brother John. Grandma Snyder, a powerful disciplinarian, stood the boys face to face, saying to Dad, "Now you ask John's forgiveness."

Glowering at his brother, Dad mumbled, "Will you?"

"Will I what?" John countered.

"What she said," Dad answered.

The apostle Paul, in his great love chapter, writes that love "keeps no records of wrongs" (1 Cor. 13:5 NIV). Does that mean "forgive and forget"? Some years back, concerned about my attitude toward a missionary colleague, I felt impelled to write him a letter and ask forgiveness. He replied, "There is no problem. I have no resentment. I have 'built-in' forgiveness." That was a new concept for me. In fact, I found it hard to believe. This colleague has now gone to heaven, but that concept of built-in forgiveness has stayed with me.

If Christians could forgive, would we still have church splits, divorces, lifelong resentments against our parents or a sibling? Perhaps, but certainly a lot less. I think forgiveness is similar to love, in that it comes in many different degrees and varied hues.

As missionaries we lived on a mission compound in designated housing, sharing cars, running errands or shopping for each other in town, dividing up mission budgets, and deciding on policy—a type of communal living. It was not easy, and mission meetings were often tense as we sometimes locked horns. As with Paul and Barnabas, the dissension was often so great that it threatened division.

One time as I was pondering an irreconcilable difference, I asked myself, "What do you do when good men disagree?" I could not come to a suitable answer. Finally, I settled on this solution: concentrate on the words "good men" and forget the part about disagreeing. Table the disagreement, think about the fact that your colleague is a good man, and try to walk around the problem some way. Many times, sometimes years later, you wonder, "What was all that monkey business about, anyway?" Time had healed the division.

What would "built-in" forgiveness be like? Forgiveness has been a difficult concept for me to grasp. To forgive one's self is often the hardest form of forgiveness. I doubt we can really rest in God's forgiveness until we have forgiven ourselves. I look back at some of the things I've done and blush, wishing things had been different. Still suffering, still wondering if I could by some means undo them. Wondering if Jesus' blood really covers them all. But 1 Corinthians 13 says that "love keeps no record of wrongs." It also adds that "love never fails." And the apostle John writes over and again, "God is love." So if love keeps no record of wrongs and God is love, then God must keep no record of wrongs, and certainly not when I have prayed for His forgiveness.

The New Testament seems to teach the concept of "built-in forgiveness."

Wasn't Jesus demonstrating this when He said on the cross, "Father, forgive them, for they know not what they do"? When the martyr Stephen was being stoned, he prayed as he was dying that God not hold this sin against them. Did he really mean that? How could God not hold that sin against them? I doubt that Stephen was just putting on an act, thinking, "This is the way Jesus died, so I should do the same thing."

Built-in forgiveness is what Jesus and Stephen were manifesting! John Wesley taught the concept of "prevenient grace." That referred to a type of grace that is active before the sinner comes to God, a type of grace, like gravity, that pulls us to Him. Sounds like built-in forgiveness to me.

Jesus taught us to pray, "Forgive us our sins as we forgive those who sin against us." Yet some of us go through life not forgiving. Deep down we have complexes and attitudes based on our reactions toward our parents. I trained in a hospital where my dad was on the staff. A colleague in surgical residency, after operating with my dad, said to me, laughing, "Al, I have finally figured out what's wrong with you. You have been an intern all your life." We both laughed, knowing that an intern was the lowest form of life in our training program. Inside, I wondered, "Wow, does it show that much?"

On the mission field our Volunteers In Service Abroad (VISA) missionaries are technically responsible to the mission superintendent. I remember two situations when a VISA missionary collided with my authority as mission superintendent. One, in frustration and near tears, said, "Well, I never got along with my dad, and you remind me of my dad." When I seemed to rub one medical student the wrong way, her sibling explained, "She never got along well with our father, and you have a lot of the characteristics of our dad."

So, should we go through life shadowboxing with parents, maybe long after they are gone? Or rebelling against authority? We are now adults; should we not forgive and forget and move on without our conditioned reflexes of anger and unforgiveness forever cropping up?

What if we are faced with something too big to forgive? Like a spouse who has forsaken his or her vows. Or a situation like the genocide in Rwanda, in which a person could run into acquaintances who very likely participated in the slaying of his family. A friend of ours returned to claim his father's house and was told, in effect, "Finders keepers, losers weepers." He concluded his life would be in danger if he pursued it further. I recall an entry from my journal written in Kigali, on September 22, 1995:

"In the p.m. Gilbauds came for tea at the Rawsons'. We got several interesting stories from these old war-horse saints—Peter on a cane from a stroke and Elizabeth looking very old They told us of their house girl, a Christian and widow of some years (with a family) who was raped during the atrocities and got pregnant, then birthed a baby boy, but the family named him 'Tumukunde' (Let us love him)." On top of this, recently, while this lady was away, her own worker robbed her and stole all the money she had saved for her children's education.

If God can change peoples' hearts to forgive such atrocities, can He not give me a heart with built-in forgiveness? An unforgiving heart is a weary, heavy heart. I long to be able to forgive—the big and the little things, every slight, every perceived injustice. If some things could simply be dropped into our mystery bag, never to be raised again, it would be like heaven.

Holiness and Cats

My mother was a saint; I wasn't. That made for some difficult growing-up years. Mother believed in the early Methodist doctrine of holiness. That meant being saved and sanctified. From the time I left the womb until she left us for a better world at age eighty-three, she never changed. Never did I see her angry, never did she yell at anyone, never did I see her do a dishonest thing, never was she disrespectful to our dad. If she did do any sinning it was probably worrying, but who wouldn't worry while rearing three sons and a daughter, especially when I was among them? Being holy isn't easy.

Holiness means different things to different people. Our church, the Free Methodist, is a "holiness" church. One doctor said to me: "Free Methodists? I know about them; they are holy rollers. They used to have camp meetings near where I grew up." That is not quite the concept we like to be known by. But we are of the Wesleyan-Arminian tradition, as is the United Methodist Church. We have always taught there are two definite works of grace, salvation and sanctification. Years ago, those of us unable to testify to being sanctified almost felt as if we were not complete Christians. It was like being on the second team in sports. Hebrews 12:14 was quoted to us: "Pursue peace with all people, and holiness, without which no one will see the Lord." One denomination affiliated with ours threw the term "second-blessing holiness" around so glibly that it sounded as if everyone in their group had *it*. In spite of these negative vibrations, the concept remained for me a glorious ideal and logical for anyone who was a follower of Jesus. At our annual conferences, our presiding bishops preached great sermons on the subject. They always made it plain that you could have an experience characterized by purity of motives and not some kind of angelic perfection. (Perfect love, the Wesleys called it.) We were admonished to make a complete and total surrender to all the known will of God.

Among some of my devout, godly friends of other denominations with different interpretations of Scripture, I perceived a tendency to laugh at our position. They referred to us as believers in perfectionism. This seemed unfair to me, as I have never known anyone who testified to being perfect. In our effort to follow Wesley's teaching on the truth that "perfect love that casts out fear" (1 John 4:18), we have gotten the reputation of teaching "sinless perfection." I do know that we believe we should and can live without willful, intentional sin, or rebellion toward God. Most true Christians agree that is what they also strive for. How could a true Christian willfully trample on or ignore God's commands?

In a little book written for The Navigators, *The Pursuit of Holiness*, Jerry Bridges writes: "God has made provision for our holiness, and He has also given us a responsibility for it...God's provision for us consists in delivering us from the reign of sin, uniting us with Christ, and giving us the indwelling Holy Spirit to reveal sin, to create a desire for holiness, and to strengthen us in our pursuit of holiness. Through the power of the Holy Spirit and according to the new nature He gives, we are to put to death the misdeeds of the body."[2]

Some people claim the experience of holiness yet do not manifest the simple fruits of the Spirit. One missionary used to say, "Before I came to the mission field I knew I was no angel, but I was surprised to learn nobody else was either." Missionaries, in my opinion, are the crème de la crème. I felt very honored to be among them, yet I have known a few who made me wonder about their definition of holiness. I told one of our mission executives that one of the interviewing questions for missionary candidates should be, "Do you ever lose your temper? And if so, how long has it been since you lost your temper?" He laughingly replied that our church doctrine does not allow for such a question. I insisted, doctrine or no doctrine, it was a very practical question that should be asked. In Galatians 5:19-20, along with all the grossest of sins, Paul lists "discord, jealousy, fits of rage, selfish ambition, dissensions, and factions." In African culture, to become angry to the point of being out of control was to act the way pagans act when they injure or murder someone. For them anger was a terrifying thing to witness. Rarely did they express anger so that it could be detected.

I recall reading once that we should not testify to being sanctified because our lives testify for us. Better to have someone come to you and ask, "What makes you like you are? How is it that you are the way I would expect Jesus to be?" Then we can tell them about what has transpired in our heart.

In a wonderful little book, *Abide in Christ*, Andrew Murray gives a description of holiness, sanctification, and the deeper life. He was a citizen of South Africa who did his theological studies in the Netherlands before becoming a minister in the Dutch Reformed Church of South Africa. He was the moderator of this Calvinist denomination for many years. He was born in 1828 and was a contemporary of D.L. Moody. His study of Scripture led him to the concept of a deeper life experience, available for anyone who followed God's leading. He eventually became a frequent speaker at the Keswick conferences in England. Somehow he managed to use only biblical terms and Scriptures and did not use any of the trigger words that seem to excite and promote opposition. He was accepted among his Calvinistic peers as well as among the followers of Wesley. He proved to me what I have always suspected, that all sincere students of the Scriptures will experientially come out at the same place, even though their minds and loyalty to traditions cannot harmonize completely.

Oswald Chambers' writings in *My Utmost for His Highest* are another example. He avoids controversial words that throw people into doctrinal conniptions. His book is timeless.

In reading biographies of outstanding Christians of the past you can frequently come upon a story of a dying to self and infilling of the Spirit that took place subsequent to salvation. George Mueller's experience is one of those: "There was a day when I died, utterly died, died to George Mueller, his opinions, preferences, tastes, and will—died to the world, its approval or censure—died to the approval or blame even of my brethren and friends—and since then I have studied only to show myself approved unto God."[3] When one goes through this death process, and emptying of self, God is able to rule in the heart without a rival.

Before we arrived in Africa we were told we must have a cat to keep rats out of the house, especially the storeroom.

"But I am a cat-hater," I protested.

This experienced missionary simply replied, "Well, if you prefer rats to cats, that is your business."

There is something about slinky cats that come up close, rub against my leg, jump up into my lap, stand, turn around, and whisk their tail in my face that I hate! I was determined to live without a cat. It was not long before I realized that I hated rats much worse than cats, but still I was resistant. I kept our dog on the back porch, letting him in the kitchen now and then when there were signs of rats. Eventually, I would have to swallow my pride and go beg a fellow missionary to let me borrow Midnight, a big, black, no-nonsense feline who brooked no foolishness from rats.

I remember the first time Midnight and I went into battle together. As usual, the houseboys were gone, it was evening, my wife had the kitchen doors all shut, and I was appointed chief rat hunter. "It is under the cabinet," I was told. So I pulled the cabinet out, and Mr. Rat darted across and under the stove. A stick under the stove drove him up into the interior of the stove. Midnight was beginning to forgive me for my antipathy and was all alert, ready to close in. I opened the oven door, and out jumped Mr. Rat. Midnight jumped into the air, twisted his body, lowered his head, and grabbed the rat between his powerful rat-crunching jaws. I praised him gratefully and allowed him to enjoy his meal before cleaning up the mess and returning him to his quiet repose in the living room of my fellow missionary.

As I reflected on this incident, I thought, "Hmm. If I had God so completely living in and taking command of my heart, no sin could dwell there." It would be like having Midnight in our storeroom and kitchen, always in charge. Midnight and rats were mutually exclusive. When the Holy Spirit takes over, other things go out.

God and sins of any kind cannot reside in the same dwelling. It is this type of abiding that Andrew Murray writes about in *Abide in Christ*. It is letting His presence completely rule our heart and abide there. Murray states that if God can do this for us for a moment, then we must trust Him for the next moment, and the next, and each succeeding hour. It is a case of allowing Him to abide permanently.

Jesus is like a lion, the king of the beasts, the strongest of the cats. Revelation 5:5 reads, "See, the Lion of the tribe of Judah, the Root of David, has triumphed" (NIV).

And my heart cries out to Him, "Jesus, come; rule in my heart. Keep all these ratty things out, because they are afraid of You!"

In my life, somewhat like George Mueller's, I have experienced that death and resurrection process, but I have to experience it again and again, or the rats dash back in and hide. Unless the Holy Spirit— like Midnight—is in control, the rats lie concealed. I can keep them from showing up most of the time, like when visitors are around, but sooner or later, they peek out from their hiding places again.

The words have now been changed, but years ago our Free Methodist Book of Discipline asked preachers being received into ordination the following:

Question: Do you believe in Christian perfection?
Question: Have you attained to this rich experience in your own heart? (If not) Are you groaning after it?

I never had to answer those questions, even though I went through the ordination process to join the Rwanda Conference of the Free Methodist Church. I had expected the questions, and pondered how I would answer.

To the first question I would have answered, "Yes, as I understand it." But I also would have had to answer the second, "I am still groaning after it."

"As the deer pants for the water brooks, so pants my soul for You, O God. My soul thirsts for God, for the living God" (Ps. 42:1-2). Most sincere Christians I know, from all traditions, feel the same way.

The Presence

A Christian artist, Nathan Greene, depicts medical scenes with Jesus standing in the background. Jesus' hands are on the shoulders of the doctor, patient, or family member. These are moving scenes. Even though we would hope that the doctor always knows his business and what to do, there are times the best of them have reached their limit of ideas, answers, and judgment. We hear prayers for the sick followed with prayers for the doctors, that they might have wisdom, that their hands will be guided by an unseen presence.

In my early years of surgical practice in the U.S., a pastor's widow, the mother of a missionary in Africa, came into my office complaining of abdominal pain. Examination revealed an ominous mass. A colon x-ray confirmed cancer of the large intestine. She was a thin, wiry little lady, very feisty, a diabetic, and in the senior category. It was nice of her to choose me for her doctor, but it put a real burden on me. She had known me since I was a boy; she knew my family and I knew hers. I had her checked by an internist; her diabetes was controlled and well managed, so I scheduled the operation at a time when my senior partner could help. Every eventuality seemed to be covered.

The morning of surgery my partner had an operation scheduled in another hospital. I was to scrub with him in the morning, and he would help me with my case in the afternoon. All seemed perfect, but problems began to arise. First, we ran into complications that prolonged his case into the afternoon. I had to leave him and go to the other hospital to start my case on time. As I arrived there I found I had one junior resident for an assistant, since it was anticipated my partner would be with me.

As we were scrubbing, and the patient was being anesthetized, the anesthesiologist said to me, "You don't plan on doing much on this case, do you?"

I replied, "Why not?"

"The chest x-ray report says the lung fields show scattered 'snowballs,' indicative of metastatic disease," she answered.

I could not believe this. The internist had approved her; I thought I had looked at the x-ray but could not be sure. It was too late to leave and go down to x-ray and discuss it, and besides, I thought, "There has to be some mistake; it is always best to get the primary out anyway, so I am going to attack this as though we are going for a cure."

The operation went very well; we found no obvious metastasis to the liver. We did a wide resection for cancer. We found a gall bladder full of large stones, but she had never had problems, so I ignored that, finished the operation, and closed up.

As soon as I could get to the radiology department, I got the chest x-ray and went to find a radiologist. He studied the film and said, "Those shadows are not metastases; two are normal body shadows and the third one is an old benign calcification." The beginning resident in radiology had overread the film, and it was typed up without a senior radiologist going over it. What a relief. To think I could have done a limited resection without trying for a cure and later learned that there had been no spread to the lungs.

I had a good feeling about how everything had gone. The anesthetist, Dr. Byrd, who had never been known for being very complimentary, commented to my partner the next day on how well the case had gone. That made me happy; I had been impressed too, as to how well everything went. I thought either God was guiding my hand and head, or He had some special concern about this particular little lady.

Then came the uncomfortable days of IVs and naso-gastric tube suction with a tube through the nose. My little lady got a bit tired of it all and started teasing me with little remarks and retorts. The day after her tubes were taken out and she was eating and looking good, she said to me, "Doctor, why do I hurt here on the other side? I know you must have left a pair of scissors in there."

To this I said, "If I did, don't worry about it; I can get another pair." And so we began to trade such remarks until the day she was to go home.

Then she teared up and said with a breaking voice, "Oh, doctor, I owe my life to you."

To this I replied, "No, you don't! You owe your life to God. You owe me dollars." She lived for around twenty more years and died of something unrelated to her cancer.

We tend to think there has to be an unseen presence, the only explanation for why something worked out as it did. Perhaps we even get a little angry with God when it does not go the way we wished, but most of us can remember many experiences when an unseen presence was palpable. Sometimes it is as though Jesus is walking to us through the storm, in the darkness, on troubled seas (Matt. 14:25). The storms are our troubles, the darkness our perplexity at having no answers. The troubled seas may even be of our own making. We cry out for help. A presence moves in, saying, "Peace." Sometimes it may be at the time of a big decision; we fear going ahead, and we fear staying put. At these times we can say, like Peter in the storm, "Lord, if it is You, command me come" (Matt. 14:28). Or if we fear moving ahead on our own and require some assurance, like Moses we can say, "If Your Presence does not go with us, do not bring us up from here" (Ex. 33:15). Then He assures us He will go with us.

That presence often comes when I have felt most alone, baffled, with no sure path ahead. When I was eighteen at Fort Ord, California, during World War II, I was lying on an upper bunk in a darkened barracks. As infantry riflemen, we were being readied for imminent departure for the Pacific theater. A deep fear seized me. A friend from our church, Virgil Ewing, had been recently killed in Europe. Several high school friends were already dead. Suddenly, my mind reasoned, "Looks like almost every family is going to lose one son. I am surely the one from our family." Soon this Scripture flashed into my mind: "Lo, I am with you always, even to the end of the age." But my memory remembered it as "even to the end of the earth."

That slight change fit right into my troubled mind, and God's presence moved into that barracks with me, surrounding me, lifting me. From then on I never knew fear, not on the troop ship as we were escorted through dangerous areas by destroyers and not during the sixteen months in the Philippine Islands where the war soon came to an end. I was always aware of that presence.

It was in high school that I had first experienced the presence. At that time I was struggling to be a Christian in my own strength, powerless to follow God. In the basement of our home I cried out to God to give me strength to walk the Christian walk. While on my knees I reached up to heaven and felt as though God reached down and grasped my hand. I prayed, "My hand is in Yours." It was very real to me. From then on when temptation came I would simply breathe a prayer, "My hand is in Yours." I was able to believe that God was reaching down to keep me from falling.

God's presence comes in our darkest moments, when we see no pathway through. Sometimes we do not recognize Him, as was the case with the disciples on the road to Emmaus. He comes along beside us, talks with us, convinces us, encourages us. Later we have to say, "Did not our heart burn within us while He talked to us on the road?" (Luke 24:32). Or we may look back as Jacob did at Bethel and say, "Surely the Lord is in this place, and I did not know it" (Gen. 28:16).

A professor at Spring Arbor University once related this incident. His wife had left for work. He was sitting alone in his home, deeply distressed over the chronic illness of his son. Suddenly he heard the outside door open and suspected his wife had forgotten something, but she did not appear. As he waited expectantly, he seemed to see a form enter the room where he sat in deep agony and despair. He looked at the form that entered, and it spoke to him. A voice said, "It will be all right." Then it left. The presence had come to give him comfort and hope in a low moment of his life.

How do we explain such apparitions? I have no answer. I only know they can be so real that we never doubt them. Scripture affirms them, as at the time Elijah was so down that he wanted God to let him die. God spoke to him in "a still small voice" (1 Kings 19:12). As it says in Isaiah 30:21, "Your ears shall hear a word behind you, saying, 'This is the way, walk in it whenever you turn to the right hand or...to the left.'"

He appears even "when the doors are shut and says 'Peace be with you'" (John 20:19). We hear Christians tell how in their bereavement and pain they were conscious of a deep inner peace in the midst of sorrow, as they "walk through the valley of shadow of death" (Ps. 23:4). Or we feel the presence, as Moses did, "in the thick darkness where God was" (Ex. 20:21).

Sometimes in moments of obscurity I grope for that presence to light my way. In faith I recall the words of this hymn:

Lead kindly Light, amid the encircling gloom.
Lead thou me on; the night is dark, and I am far from home,
Lead thou me on. Keep thou my feet; I do not ask to see the
    distant scene;
One step is enough for me.

So long thy pow'r hath blessed me, sure it still
Will lead me on o'er moor and fen, o'er crag and torrent, till
The night is gone. And with the morn those angel faces smile.
Which I have loved long since, and lost awhile.

—John H. Newman

I follow that light—the light of His presence. I have learned God is never far away.

A Call

S ister Miriam was not like any other Catholic nun I had known. I had known a few during medical school and while working as an emergency room physician at St. Mary's Hospital, but this one was young and vivacious; you could even describe her as pretty. She had been a laboratory technician in Belgium before becoming a religious. We were honored to be entrusted by the mother superior, Mère Laurentine, and the neighboring Catholic mission to provide Sister Miriam with a six-week medical rotation at our Kibogora Hospital.

Early on, we learned that Sister Miriam was not with us for fun and games. It had seemed only polite to invite her to our coffee breaks, at our houses, at 10 each morning. We would have had her come for lunch too, but her order insisted that she carry her own lunch and eat it in one of the offices at the hospital. In spite of her gray habit, with its head covering and its train down the back of her neck, our nurses soon felt a real kinship with her. She was immediately attracted to the piano in our house. She told us how she loved to play and of the years she had spent becoming a pianist. Of course we wanted her to play for us, but, uncomplainingly, she told us that this was not permitted during the year of her novitiate.

One day she shared with us how she had chosen the Order of the Benedictine Sisters in Rwanda. She had wanted to become a missionary but did not know much about the different orders. As she learned about some, she narrowed it down to four choices. But how was she to know which one God was calling her to? As a postulant, she struggled with this. She had prayed, but no definite answer had come. Soon she would have to make a decision. Then a novel idea hit her.

Sister Miriam wrote the name of each of the four orders on separate pieces of paper. With each paper she made a paper airplane. Then, with a prayer, she sailed them, one by one, at the crucifix. The one that landed the closest to the crucifix—nearest to Jesus' feet— would be the one God had obviously ordained for her. Well, the one she wanted the least, the Order of the Benedictine Sisters, landed the closest to Jesus. Voila! Sister Miriam's call to Rwanda.

I have heard of many different types of "calls," but Sister Miriam's struck me as about the strangest and perhaps most novel. Later, I recalled that when the early disciples of Jesus wanted to replace Judas and bring their number back to the original twelve, they had written several names on slips of paper, prayed about the matter, and drew lots. Wasn't Sister Miriam's method every bit as good?

We did not learn a whole lot more about Sister Miriam, because when the mother superior learned that she was participating in our coffee breaks she told her to spend the time in meditation, not in frivolity.

Sister Miriam was eventually placed at a distant mission near the town of Butare. Sometimes, we would see her walking along the road with another sister, or even in a pickup truck traveling somewhere. We would stop and exchange pleasantries, or wave as we passed. She always seemed very happy and fulfilled in what she was doing.

So what is a call? I was amused at the varied reactions of people when they heard I was going to Africa. One surgeon, who in my opinion had respect for neither God nor man and who believed all learning had to be painful—punctuating his belief by making my life extra painful every time I scrubbed with him—once said, "If Al's called, he had better go!" Another doctor, a friend of my dad's who had known me from childhood, looked me straight in the eye and said, "Al, I thought you had better sense."

An amusing song, which I won't call a hymn, portrays the singer arguing with God; the refrain at the end of each verse pleads,

"Please don't send me to Africa." But I say, why not? Is having a call a terrible sentence? Was Sister Miriam serving time, some kind of penance for her sins? Or was she one of the most fortunate people on earth?

After reading Tom Brokaw's *The Greatest Generation*, in which he describes my generation—those who went through the depression, World War II, and lived through the post-war years—I realized that my thinking had been molded by an entirely different set of events than that of my children and the baby boomer generation. I tell my children, "My generation grew up asking themselves, 'What am I supposed to do with my life? To what am I called?' Your generation asks itself, 'What do I want to do? What would be fun? What am I interested in?'"

In Dr. David Burn's best-selling book, *Feeling Good* (which for the most part I heartily recommend), one of the cognitive distortions he lists is the use of "should" statements. We are advised to avoid such words as "should, ought, must, have to, shouldn't" and so forth. Of course we all struggle with false guilt, but the apostle Paul said, "Woe is me, if I do not preach the gospel." Maybe he needed counseling. My mother used a lot of "should and should not" statements on me. I wondered if I was suffering from child abuse.

Sometimes it is a great comfort to have someone tell us what we ought to do, or at least what they think we ought to do. A passage from *Alice in Wonderland* is often cited as an example of this. Alice asks the Cheshire cat, "Would you tell me, please, which way I ought to go from here?"

"That depends a good deal on where you want to get to," said the cat.

"I don't much care where," said Alice.

"Then it doesn't matter which way you go," said the cat.

I wonder what the Cheshire cat would have said if Alice had answered, "I want to go the right way." For me, and any other Christian, there is a right way and a wrong way, a narrow way and a broad way. For every Christian Jesus' words are plain: "Follow Me."

When we first appeared before our mission board for questioning, I was asked to tell about my call. After I finished, my wife was asked, "Now, Mrs. Snyder, tell us about your call."

Louise answered very clearly and definitely, "My call is to go where my husband feels he should go."

We wondered how that was going to fly, but it so happened that the chairman of the board did not like to go anywhere without his wife. He immediately and readily accepted that response and in years to come loved to quote it to others. You would be hard-pressed to find any Scripture that did not substantiate her answer.

At weddings, we eulogize Ruth (in the Old Testament) and her words to her mother-in-law Naomi: "Entreat me not to leave you... wherever you go, I will go...wherever you lodge, I will lodge...your people shall be my people, and your God, my God...where you die, I will die" (Ruth 1:16-17). Wedding vows follow New Testament principles to love, honor, and cherish (or obey, depending on your understanding of Scripture). My point is, it is not too hard to know the "right way," if your rules are based on Scripture.

In Rwanda, a missionary retreat was held every July. Around two hundred missionaries from many missions and several countries would gather for ten days of fellowship. On the last Saturday evening all the new missionaries were asked to tell their story, which usually meant "tell about your call." One young doctor, who had first come as a medical student and had returned as a missionary, asked to talk to me. He began, "I am supposed to tell about my call this Saturday night, but I don't know what to say. I never felt that I had a real call."

"Well, Tom, why did you come back here?" I asked.

I loved his answer; it was so honest and clear, and made a call sound so simple.

"Well," he said, "I had seen the need. I thought that I had the ability to meet that need. And I thought it would please God for me to try to do that."

"That's all you have to say." I told him. How could any call be clearer or simpler?

For many of us, our call comes as a response to a restlessness and a desire to be in a special relationship with God. St. Augustine said, "Our hearts are restless until they can find peace in You." My first exposure to missions, and the so-called Third World, was in the Philippine Islands. I stayed for over a year after the actual fighting of

World War II ended. I was among the last to arrive, so I was among the last to go home. Here I first felt the call. That experience and exposure to mission work put a restlessness in me that never would go away.

As a doctor, my experience in Burundi ruined me forever for working in the United States. I was working with a group of six doctors in Grand Rapids. I had qualified as a senior surgeon, and the group I was working with invited me to a meeting.

"You have now been with us two years," I was told. "We are inviting you to join the corporation as a full partner. This will mean more to you financially. You will be under all our benefits, for retirement, et cetera."

It took me no time at all to reply. "I thank you very much and appreciate being asked to join you," I said. "I can still hear the drumbeats of Africa. I intend to eventually go back there. If it is all right with you, I will remain in my present status until the time that I go back."

They accepted this.

By the drumbeats in Africa, I meant I was marching to a different drummer than they were. For me, it was a bit like Jack London's *Call of the Wild*. John Thornton's dog, Buck, would periodically leave his master and run with the wolves, first killing small game, then a bear, and eventually a bull moose. Always, he would come back to his beloved master, but the call of the wild was in his heart and genes. Eventually, after the death of Thornton, Buck left forever, answering that imperious call of the wild. Occasionally he would be sighted running at the head of the wolf pack.

In 1968, while at a Sunday morning church service shortly after my return to Africa, I looked at the hymnbook and wondered who had learned this language well enough to translate these songs. I marveled at the entire Bible translated into Kinyarwanda. What a tremendous task! The bricks, made at the mission, were neatly patterned on the floor and walls; I was gripped with awe while gazing at the beams forming the high roof structure. As the African pastor ended his sermon, the singing began. I watched the pastors inviting people forward to pray. And I wondered who had trained these pastors.

As people came forward in large numbers to become disciples of Jesus, I experienced a moment of epiphany, as I realized that this was God's kingdom coming upon the earth. I had perceived something of what it had taken to bring it to pass, and most of all, I realized that I was part of it all. My plans had fused with God's purposes.

Often as we respond to the call, God gives us little perceptions of His presence. One time, we were traveling through Tanzania on the way to Mwanza and the Serengeti. One day's journey from Kigali, we stopped for lodging at the isolated Catholic Mission of Biharamula. We had been traveling through forlorn and wild country. With no stores and no hotels anywhere nearby, this place was a refuge. After a shower and while waiting for supper, with the daylight receding, I wandered into the church. More ornate than our Protestant churches, it was still rather simple. It was a bit chilly, gloomy, and silent, but I noted some birds nesting in the rafters and flying around the ceiling. The words of Psalm 84 came to mind. "Even the sparrow has found a home, and the swallow a nest for herself, where she may lay her young—even Your altars, O Lord of hosts." My heart was suddenly in tune with that psalm and the preceding verse. "My soul longs, yes even faints for the courts of the Lord; my heart and my flesh cry out for the living God" (Psalm 84:2 & 3). And my heart exulted in the realization that like the sparrow and swallow, God had a place for me!

Trudging up the hill after a day at the hospital, I often reflected upon the day. After saving a mother in shock from a ruptured uterus, or relieving the pain of a neglected fracture, or just watching the staff we had trained, functioning with competence, there came a great joy. Then I could breathe a prayer, "Lord, my heart is no longer restless; it has found its peace in You. Thank You for calling me."

A call can be summed up in the title to Betty Ellen Cox's book *Simply Following*. We are all called to follow Jesus. There is really no "part-time" or "full-time" Christian service, nor a special call, to special people, to special places. On the road to Damascus, Paul answered, "Lord, what do you want me to do?" (Acts 9:6). We can ask the same thing. In listening and following, we find our special place. And here we find peace.

Blood

Nestled in a valley in the mountains of Rwanda, three degrees south of the equator and far from any city, lies Kibogora Hospital. Nestled in a valley, its small staff of doctors, nurses, and technicians battle the grim reaper on a daily basis. Most of the time we win. Many things we can do without, but it is a constant struggle doing surgery without enough blood. Often the doctor can get by with intravenous saline solutions or blood substitutes. But sometimes he must have blood. I was blessed with a relatively rare blood type—B positive. Since it was unlikely that a surgical patient would have that same blood type, this spared me from an ethical dilemma: should I or should I not give my own blood and try to operate at the same time?

Our mission borders on Lake Kivu, one of the great lakes of Africa. Directly off the compound, a road continues up the mountain to a small village called Rangiro. Here a Swiss forestry project was in operation. Adrian Sommers, a Swiss forester, and his wife, Susan, were friends of ours. Susan, only twenty-two, was seeing me for prenatal care during her first pregnancy. All was going well. I had cross-matched her blood with that of her husband. They were both O positive.

The day she went into labor, all seemed to be normal; labor progressed normally and she gave birth to a beautiful baby girl. While sewing up the episiotomy I noted more bleeding than usual. I routinely checked the cervix, though I felt that was an unlikely source. Finished with the sewing, I began to search for the source of the bleeding. I sent for my surgical nurse, Rosa, to help me make a more thorough examination for cervical tears. None were found.

So, we did the usual things—another injection of ergotamine, an oxytocin drip intravenously—but still the bleeding was too brisk. The uterus was not contracting down; after massaging and applying abdominal pressure the uterus would lose its firm contracted feeling, going limp and boggy. We took turns, with the missionary nurses squeezing down on the uterus through the lower abdomen. After each attempt, further bleeding would ensue. Susan's pulse became rapid, and her blood pressure dropped. In desperation we drew blood from Adrian, a strong, healthy forester. We gave it to Susan, then continued to watch her for another hour; blood continued to ooze. One of the missionary nurses, also O positive, volunteered her blood, so we drew a pint from Sheryl. By this time I had done a cut-down on an ankle vein and inserted a catheter into the saphenous vein. We gave dextran and artificial blood expanders of gelatin, barely keeping up with the blood loss.

As a last resort, I decided to do what they had taught us back in medical school—pack the uterus with sterile gauze. In recent years it was thought to be a bit dangerous and was said to only conceal hemorrhage, but I had no other option. I packed the uterus, and with constant manual pressure on the uterus the hemorrhage seemed controlled. We stabilized Susan but still considered surgery. I feared racing against the hemorrhage, using surgery to see who could win—the surgeon or the bleeding. At this point, I sent Walter Silver, a non-medical missionary, off to Mugonero, a mission hospital a ninety-minute drive away. Walt carried a note to a colleague to come help me. My plan was to remove the packing, and then, if the hemorrhage persisted, we would have to do a hysterectomy.

By now, it was midnight; our diesel generator had been running all evening. We shut it down, and I went home to get a little sleep, while the nurses—missionary and national— watched over Susan. Sleep eluded me. Finally, at about 4 a.m., I heard the Land Rover bumping down the road to the hospital.

I was scared, my mouth as dry as cotton, my own pulse as rapid as Susan's, and my blood pressure twice as high as hers. I felt that if Susan died, I would just as soon die too. It was something I could not face. My colleague and I dressed for surgery. The instruments were all prepared, and the national surgical team was ready. First, we would remove the uterine packing, hoping and praying that surgery would not be necessary.

Susan remained incredibly calm and cooperative. Even Adrian appeared calm. With a nurse palpating the uterine fundus I gently teased out the pack. *No bleeding!* We waited; the uterus stayed firm. The bleeding did not start again. Unbelievable! We watched expectantly, *the hemorrhage had stopped!*

Some of us went off for an early morning breakfast. We moved Susan to a hospital bed across from my office and watched her carefully all that day. That evening we brought her up to a guest room in our house. Here she stayed for seven days, gradually gaining strength and becoming better able to get along without intravenous solutions or more blood. Before allowing her to go home, I did another hemoglobin. She had seven grams, about one-half of what a normal person should have. This was one week later and after receiving two transfusions. It confirmed to me what a major hemorrhage it had been.

Blood is precious. We can't live without it. Before people knew anything about physiology they knew that bleeding an animal or a man would result in death. The Bible states that the life is in the blood (Lev. 17:11).

Getting members of the African staff to donate blood was not easy, especially if they were not related to the patient. I had to reason with the fervor of an evangelist. I would offer to pay very well, something close to several days' pay. But they would counter, "What good will the money do me if I die?" I gave them the scientific facts: they had nine or ten pints of blood, they could lose three pints before they began to feel symptoms, the body starts to remake blood immediately, and in two weeks it would be totally replaced. I promised a large bottle of Coke, assuring them that the fluid would start to replace itself. Jokingly, I said we would replace the blood with Coke. No one was impressed. I read somewhere that this reluctance was based on the belief that to give your blood to another was to give them power over you. I noticed that it was not difficult to get blood from a near relative. That made me suspect this explanation might be valid.

Now and then I would find someone who was not afraid to give blood. A worker on the building crew named Hesron was one of these. He was O positive. We typed blood with Eldon Cards from Sweden. These were good for typing as well as giving a card to the donor for future reference. Periodically, I would send for Hesron and ask him to give blood. He always was willing. Amazing! I wanted to keep Hesron on our building crew forever, but one day he said he was going to Uganda to seek work. That was a bad day for the hospital. We only had a couple others who were willing to help in emergencies.

Some years later, a bedraggled, very poor-looking man approached me and asked for work. I was busy and brushed him off with, "Go talk to the foreman." He got nowhere, so he came back and kept bugging me. Each time, I pushed him away. Finally, one afternoon one of my staff came to me and handed me an Eldon Card, saying, "There is a man outside looking for work. He asked me to show you this card." I looked at the Eldon Card very curiously and soon spotted the name of Hesron, who turned out to be the poor man. "Oh," I said, "tell him to come in." From then on my "blood brother" Hesron had steady employment at our hospital.

Very few people enjoy the sight of blood. My brother-in-law leaves the room if our doctor family gets too vivid in our description of a day's work. Many medical students have gotten the "vapors" while observing certain procedures during their early days in medicine. While I was practicing in Grand Rapids my neighbor's son needed some stitches. With his father, I took the boy down to the emergency room. The father wanted to watch. I was reluctant, so I asked him if he had ever seen stitches being put in. He assured me he had—many times. I took the precaution of having him sit down. Then, he confidently assured me he had watched such things "many times, but on television." Just as I began to work, the nurse had to help him out of the room "to get some air."

Another friend told about a time in an emergency room when he was "helping" by standing beside his son. The room got hot, his head began to swim, and he ended up sitting in a wheelchair in the hall. His final humiliation came when the nurse asked him if he would like a Popsicle.

Blood is fascinating. The gospel is built upon it. On my grandfather's tombstone is written, "Without shedding of blood there is no remission" (Heb. 9:22). Why had he chosen that? I reason that he was making no claim to salvation except for Jesus' death in his place. The Passover celebrates the children of Israel's deliverance in Egypt. They were to put a lamb's blood on the lintel of their house, and when the death angel saw the blood he would pass by that house (Ex. 12:13).

Blood carries oxygen and nourishes, cleanses, and warms us. Our bloodlines identify us. Our blood group and DNA tell all kinds of things about us. God made us this way.

Blood is very symbolic throughout the entire Bible, in both the Old and New Testaments. God provided for our salvation by it, first by animal sacrifices in the Old Testament, then by Jesus' death in the New Testament. Jesus speaks of drinking His blood and eating His body during the sacrament of communion. What does that mean? We go through the ritual often not visualizing what is being said, but without Jesus' blood atoning for our sins there is no possibility of salvation. "How shall we escape if we neglect so great a salvation?" (Heb. 2:3). Who would possibly want to neglect it? It provides for all of us a "city of refuge." The cities of refuge (Num. 35:6, Deut. 19:2-6) in the Old Testament were places where someone who had committed manslaughter or caused an unintentional death could flee and be safe from the law of an "eye for an eye, and a tooth for a tooth." (We surgeons could really use such a place. It might obviate the need to carry malpractice insurance!)

It is not only surgeons but also internists and everyone else who need an escape. In Romans 3:23 it says, "For all have sinned and fall short of the glory of God." Jesus emphasized this when He said, "He who is without sin among you, let him throw a stone at her first" (John 8:7). So, He made provision for this. "Christ was offered once to bear the sins of many. To those who eagerly wait for Him He will appear a second time, apart from sin, for salvation" (Heb. 9:28).

Hymn writers express salvation in graphic descriptions of blood:

There is a fountain filled with blood drawn from
    Immanuel's veins;
And sinners plunged beneath that flood lose all their guilty
    stains.
The dying thief rejoiced to see that fountain in his day;
And there may I, though vile as he, wash all my sins away.

—William Cowper

God gave His Son to bleed and die for our sins, and not for our sins only, but for everyone's. Parents should claim this for their children and lead them to understanding it. The invitation in our discipline reads in part, "You who truly and earnestly repent of your sins...and who intend to lead a new life, draw near with faith, and take this holy sacrament to your comfort, and humbly kneeling, make your honest confession to Almighty God."

At times, all I could say to qualify was that I was truly and earnestly sorry for my sins, and I intended to lead a new life. I feared not partaking in communion. It can represent a new start or a turning back to Christ. I love to see children taking part.

In Africa, each summer at the Kumbya missionary retreat we ended with a communion service. Some missionary kids, about twelve years or younger and from different persuasions than ours, did not participate. I was shocked as I saw them watching from the back row. Apparently they had been taught if they had not yet made their public confession of faith and undergone baptism they were not allowed to take communion. But I reason that Jesus said, "Let the little children come to Me, and do not forbid them; for of such is the kingdom of Heaven" (Matt. 19:14). In Acts 16:33, when Paul and Silas were released from prison, the Philippian jailer "and all his family were baptized."

Charles Wesley wrote this:

He ever lives above, for me to intercede
His all-redeeming love, His precious blood to plead;
His blood atoned for all our race, His blood atoned for all
our race,
And sprinkles now the throne of grace.

Water

We were in full battle; our company was attacking the enemy across a valley. It was March of 1945, and this was Arkansas. Our bullets were blank cartridges, and I was tired and a little bored. We had just run across an open area, diving behind tree trunks. I was catching my breath, my rifle lying at my side, the muzzle about eighteen inches from my face, when I saw a red ant running up the bark of the tree.

"Aha!" I thought. "Here is a chance to do some real killing." Without another thought, I reached down and pulled the trigger. In the urgency of the moment, I had forgotten about the several inches of flames and smoke that are emitted when a blank cartridge is fired. My eyes were filled with gunpowder smoke, flying particles of bark, and much pain. In my distress I could only think that I had lost my eyesight. I was afraid to open my eyes, but my first squint revealed a blur and daylight rather than darkness.

I snatched my canteen from its holster, rolled over, and poured water into my eyes. I then ran across to another tree and asked a buddy to rinse my eyes with the water that remained. The pain subsided, and I could still see. I did not require any more medical help. The water had saved my sight. Water heals!

I am often asked, "Did you get the ant?" I can only respond, "I think so."

In my early days in Burundi, I was called to see a poor, dying beggar. The dispenser who called me had put him down in an isolated hut reserved for tuberculosis patients. He was dirty and covered with lice, hands and toes neglected, with chiggers everywhere around the nails. His hair was matted. "Take him up to the hospital and put him in a bed." I said. "Oh, no, everyone would leave the hospital if I did," was the reply. I struggled with what I could do, what was right, and whether I should break custom and force them to put him in the ward. Later I went back alone to see him. He could not talk, but I propped him up and tried to put some water in his mouth. At the same time, in the little Kirundi I had learned, I tried to say, "I give you this water in the name of Jesus." The next morning he was dead. I am not proud of that case. It haunts me to this day. I know now what I would do if I had the chance to do it over. But it does illustrate that when we can't do anything else, we can at least give a cup of water in Jesus' name.

A Catholic priest in the northwest town of Gisenyi, Rwanda, traveled doing mobile clinic work. His primary objective, as a member of the order "The Friends of Father Damien," was to treat leprosy patients. He would treat all skin diseases to avoid the stigma of being known as the leprosy doctor. He was not a doctor but an *agent santaire* (sanitary agent). He had developed all kinds of theories and practical treatments that seemed to work. From him, I learned to treat scabies with crankcase oil, conserved after changing the oil in the car. It worked, but my idea of why it worked was that if you smeared the itching scabies lesions with discarded black crankcase oil, the clothes and body were so messy that just in washing it all off and washing it out of your clothes, the scabies mite would give up and get out of there or die. There again, healing water.

The "padre," as we called him, had another special treatment for leg and foot ulcers. These were seen often in Africa, especially in leprosy patients who had lost feeling in their feet. His treatment was simple and practical. He would take large rubber boots, fill them with clean water, and have the patient soak the lower leg and foot in the boot for about an hour each day. The results were truly amazing; the ulcers healed. Clean water was all that was needed.

Occasionally, we would be hit with an epidemic of cholera. It was scary. The patient would come in with typical rice-water stools. The patient would be drained of all strength, and death would rapidly ensue. Our management was a bit nauseating, but it worked well. With a cholera bed—a cot with a hole cut in it—the patient in shock would lie supine, bottom over the hole, and a bedpan or pot on the floor beneath. The relatives would empty the pot when it was full. Death would come in a very short while unless we could replace the body fluids. Patients were encouraged to drink by someone constantly offering water with salt in it. More often than not, though, it required giving the water intravenously. Our problem was to find enough intravenous fluids to keep up. We knew we could use rain-water if distilled water was not available. However, our still was too slow for our needs, and we could not find enough clean rain-water. In this life-or-death situation we took spring water, filtered it, and measured out the pure salt to make a 0.9 percent solution (nine grams of sodium chloride per liter). After sterilizing it, we used it sparingly at first, fearful of it being toxic, but the patients immedi-ately improved. We soon were hanging up the bottles, and with a large-bore needle pouring fluids into the patient, sometimes ten or twelve liters. The dispensers would change the speed as needed. If the pulse became rapid and feeble, the fluids would be speeded up; if the patient began to be alert, and the pulse was strong and slowing, the IV would be slowed down. It was miraculous. We quit losing patients. Many would be clinically well in twenty-four hours, asking to go home. Saved by water!

A statistic from a conference in Asia was recently quoted on National Public Radio: one-half billion people suffer from a chronic shortage of water. This number is eventually expected to grow to three billion.

To be without electricity would be a real handicap, I once thought. But after being in Africa I realized that a water shortage is much worse. You can use kerosene lamps or candles, or go to bed when it is dark, but what can substitute for water? Some of the most difficult crises in the mission occurred at times of water shortage. If we would not share from our reservoir we would be looked upon as selfish, inconsiderate neighbors.

Water is an essential part of our life. We start out early in life calling out from our cribs, "Dwink, dwink." As parents, we go through the drink routine by trying to balance the "Dwink, dwink" against bed-wetting problems. We learn to go through the routine prophylactically with, "First, go potty." Then, "Just a sip. Now lights out. No more!"

Warm water is soothing. On a cold, rainy night in Africa my wife would submerge herself in a hot, soothing bath and remark, "Can you imagine the refugees sleeping out on the ground in this rain under a sheet of plastic, and here we are so comfortable? It doesn't seem fair! How can I take a bath in nice, warm water when my neighbors cannot find enough to cook or drink?"

Dr. M, the minister of health, was visiting Kibogora Hospital and stayed the night in our home. On this particular night, he was suffering from a bad cold and a respiratory infection. He asked me if I had anything in our pharmacy for his cold. I did—just the thing. I went down to the hospital, bringing back a bottle of Actifed syrup, which contains lots of antihistamine. Since he was a large man, I poured him a strong dose. We visited for a while, and then he went over to our piano and played. It was a quiet, relaxed evening. Later, we showed him to his room, told him there was plenty of hot water for a bath, and retired to our room. For a while, I heard a lot of noise and splashing from the bathroom, but the noise gradually subsided, then stopped. All was deathly quiet. I said to Louise, "I wonder if he is all right." I began to recalculate the dose of Actifed I had poured for him. It seemed rather hefty, but still essentially correct. I feared he had some special sensitivity that had caused him to fall asleep. Could his head have slipped under the water? That did not seem too likely, given his size and the size of the tub, but I began to see myself being arraigned in Kigali for the death of the minister of health—guilty, and standing before the firing squad.

I screwed up my courage. Standing close to the door I listened. All was silent. Finally, I asked rather loudly, "Ministre, êtes vous bien?" (Minister, are you okay?) Then came a couple of snorts, clearing of the throat a couple of times, followed by, "Oui, je suis bien." (Yes, I'm okay.)

In the morning, he explained that he had been very weary, and the warm water had sedated him until he fell asleep in the tub. I did not elaborate on the soporific side effects of Actifed and antihistamines.

Water! Good, clear, cool, thirst-quenching water. Healing streams of water. Living water. Cool water on a fevered forehead; cooling sponge baths for fevered children. Water that rinses away dirt and infection, cleansing wounds, cleansing the hands of nurses and doctors treating cholera and dysentery. Water that restores the circulation of burned, shocked patients and dehydrated dysentery patients. Water given in a glass in Jesus' name. What would we ever do without water?

The Bible emphasizes over and over the value of water and makes analogies to God's Spirit, as in these passages:

Psalm 42:1-2: "As the deer pants for the water brooks, so pants my soul for You, O God. My soul thirsts for God, for the living God."

Isaiah 44:3: "For I will pour water on him who is thirsty, and floods on the dry ground."

Water has great significance in religious rituals:

Acts 8:36-37: The Ethiopian said to Phillip, "See, here is water. What hinders me from being baptized?" "If you believe with all your heart, you may," Phillip replied.

Isaiah 55:1: Ho! Everyone who thirsts, come to the waters.

In John 4:10, speaking with the woman of Samaria, Jesus answered and said to her, "If you knew the gift of God, and who it is who says to you, 'Give Me a drink,' you would have asked Him, and He would have given you living water." He continues, "Whoever drinks of the water that I shall give him will never thirst. But the water that I shall give him will become in him a fountain of water springing up into eternal life" (John 4:14).

Hymns are replete with references to water. One we used to sing years ago, but now almost forgotten, goes like this:

All my life long I had panted for a draught from some cool
    spring
That I hoped would quench the burning of the thirst I felt
    within.
Well of water ever springing, bread of life, so rich and free,
Untold wealth that never faileth, My Redeemer is to me.

—Clara Tear Williams

The last reference to water in the Bible is in Revelation 22:17. It is beautiful, and it is offered to all of us: "And the Spirit and the Bride say, 'Come!' And let him who hears say, 'Come!' And let him who thirsts come. Whoever desires, let him take the water of life freely."

And each one of us can look up to heaven, and like a little child, cry to the Father, "Drink, drink." And it won't be a "sip." He has promised to pour water on him who is thirsty and floods on the dry ground. Just come!

NIMBY

"NIMBY! Not in my back yard," replied an environmental expert to a question on *The Lehrer News Hour*. The actions of our government's Environment Protection Agency were being scrutinized, and she was "agin" them. I thought, "Now there is a new acronym for the English language." NIMBY makes it so simple to express a negative view. But I am confused. I thought we were in the age of tolerance. My mother used to say, "Not in this house, young man." But that was a different age. Now it's, "Whatever turns you on. Whatever floats your boat." An openly gay priest can be consecrated a bishop in the Episcopal Church, but only a minority hollers "NIMBY!"—and not enough to be heard. On the other hand, an Alabama chief justice displays an artistic sculpture of the Ten Commandments in the rotunda of the justice building, but tolerance of that is unacceptable. Higher authorities cried "NIMBY!" If it is fashionable to yell NIMBY sometimes, why isn't it at other times? Was God too negative when He gave us the Ten Commandments? Eight of the ten say NIMBY, or "Thou shalt not," to such things as adultery, stealing, lying, swearing, worshipping idols, and so forth.

In April of 1957, I witnessed an example of speaking up for right. I was beginning a hospital "stage" (required rotation) in a government hospital in Bujumbura, Burundi. Those were colonial days, and the Belgian government profited by using many Catholic sisters as charge nurses on the various services. One of my mentors was Dr. Falaise, a burly, friendly Belgian surgeon. He was full of good humor and fun to be with. He was somewhat self-made from years of battling against the odds in primitive circumstances. He would struggle through a difficult operation with poor anesthesia, in an operating room at 90 degrees Fahrenheit, and as he would put in the last stitch in the peritoneum to close the abdomen, he would breathe a sigh of relief and say, "Voila. Le drame est caché" (There. The drama is hidden).

The hospital consisted of a series of buildings, all the same size, connected by roofed open walkways forming "T's" connecting one unit to the other. In the mornings I would often meet Dr. Falaise coming down the walk. Having checked on his patient, he would yell happily to me, "Il vit toujours, confrère!" (He is still living, confrère).

There were all types working there. Besides the trim, quiet nuns bustling about in their white striped habits, white starched head covering, and white shoes were various Belgian government nurses and workers. Ms. X, a plumpish, somewhat noisy lady in her thirties, who fit Webster's description of a flapper, was a contrast to the nuns in both her skimpy attire designed to cope with the heat and her obvious lifestyle. She had three small children who walked to the hospital after school each afternoon and waited around until Ms. X finished work for the day. A certain gentleman, a bit older than she and obviously neither her husband nor the father of the children, would come by with his car and take the family home to where they all lived together.

As so often happened near the end of a hospital day, when things slow down and the day shift is looking forward to going home, one day a note arrived from the maternity saying that there was a case of delayed labor in the delivery room needing a vacuum extraction (*venteuse* in French) delivery.

Dr. Falaise turned to me and asked, "Have you ever seen a venteuse delivery?" "No," I answered.

He laughed and said, "It probably has not arrived in America yet."

The vacuum extractor was first developed in Sweden. It consists of a metal cup that fixes onto the fetal scalp as suction is built up through a rubber tube containing a small chain attached to a handle. Ms. X overheard the conversation, and looking for something to entertain her children said, "Come, kids, you can watch this venteuse delivery," explaining that the ten- and seven-year-old girls, and small boy, had never seen a venteuse delivery. I was horrified as they followed us to the maternity.

Inside the delivery room was an African lady tired out from a long labor. She was lying on the delivery table, her legs spread in supports, and of course her anatomy exposed to the public now entering the room. An African midwife was already preparing the venteuse. Dr. Falaise, ignoring everything except the delivery, was preparing for work, explaining to me all the while what he was doing. Behind me in a semicircle were Ms. X and her wide-eyed young brood. Just then a very young Belgian nun midwife walked in, took one incredulous look at the audience, and, opening the door quietly, told the kids to leave. Their mother walked over to block them and said to the nun, "I have brought them with me. They have never seen a venteuse delivery before."

"Pas dans ma salle d'accouchement" (not in my delivery room), replied the sister as she shooed the kids out the door.

Seconds later, Ms. X quietly opened the door and called the children back in. As soon as the sister spotted them, she walked over and repeated, "Pas dans ma salle d'accouchement," ushering the kids out the door another time.

Again, Ms. X let the children back in and addressed the sister. "I have gotten permission from the mother superior, and it is all right," she lied.

For a third time, the sister spread her arms, pushed the children out the door, and locked it, and in a loud stern voice, almost shouted, "Pas dans ma salle d'accouchement!"

I was watching all this with more interest than I had in the delivery by vacuum extractor. Ms. X, tired now and defeated, quietly made her exit from another door to join her children.

I felt like shouting, "Yea, Sister! You won! I'm proud of you."

Instead, I returned to observing the delivery of the baby. Eventually, I would need to do hundreds of venteuse deliveries as the lone doctor in a bush hospital in the mountains of Burundi and Rwanda.

I will never forget the calm, immovable authority of that young Belgian sister, standing up for what she believed to be right. My kids have heard the story so many times that when something in our house needed an unequivocal "No," they knew exactly what was implied when I would say, "Pas dans ma salle d'accouchement!" They even use the phrase themselves when they want to be emphatic.

It takes courage to speak up with a strong, "No way!" At a glance the sister could see that a helpless little woman was being robbed of her dignity and privacy. A sacred moment of birth was being turned into a spectacle. In addition, multiple people in the delivery room, especially children, increased the chance of infection. A woman who had come to the hospital for help was being treated casually.

So the sister, in effect, cried out, "Never! Not on my watch."

How many times do we remain silent when we know we should speak up? The Bible is replete with good examples. Consider Joseph, Moses, Daniel, and especially Esther, after hearing Mordecai's words: "For if you remain silent...deliverance will arise for the Jews from another place, but you and your father's house will perish... who knows whether you have come to the kingdom for such a time as this?" (Esther 4:14).

Integrity

For to this you were called,
because Christ also suffered for us,
leaving us an example,
that you should follow in His steps.
1 Peter 2:21

Abstain from every form of evil.
1 Thess. 5:22

A few years ago, I had the unfortunate experience of being pulled over for speeding. The sheriff who stopped me said he was putting me down for exceeding the limit by less than ten miles per hour because I had been honest with him in admitting I was actually going seventy miles per hour in a fifty-five miles-per-hour zone. That would cost me only two points on my driving record rather than what it could have been. I thanked him and drove away repentant. I vowed to change my ways, especially because my wife had often warned me about the consequences. Worse yet, my teenage grandson was in the back seat seeing it all. What an awful example, even if the sheriff did commend me for being truthful.

Would we be happy if God had put the Ten Commandments on a point system, giving a value to each one, scoring each with points on a one-to-ten basis? Subconsciously, we do that. Even though the Bible tells us that to break one law is to break all of them, we scarcely believe that. Fortunately, I am not the judge.

If I were to be scorekeeper in the game of life, I would probably assess the commandments on a scale something like this: ten points for murder, nine points for adultery, eight points for stealing, seven points for lying, same for false testimony, six points for cursing, same for dishonoring our parents, five points for having idols, four for coveting, three for Sabbath-breaking, and so on.

For me adultery has always rated high on the list of bad things, even though Jesus taught that the seemingly lesser offense of lust is really adultery in the heart. One summer, when I was a boy growing up on the farm, a dear friend of my mother's came frequently to pour out her heart over a great sorrow. Mom would join her in the car; they would drive around slowly, sometimes stopping on the shoulder of our country road to talk privately. As this began to happen more frequently, Mom explained that this lady's husband, a preacher, was having an affair with another woman. Mom was the only one she could turn to. I was incredulous. You mean, this guy was a fake, a hypocrite, a cruel betrayer, and all the terrible names I could attach to him? This man whose family had been our friends for years?

Years later Mom phoned to tell me of another disaster. This one was like an incurable cancer and had struck closer to home. Dad's youngest sister, more like a sister to me than an aunt, was now the victim of betrayal by her spouse. As the story unraveled, I felt as if I had been hit in the stomach. My reaction was that he had not only betrayed her but had also betrayed our entire family. Everyone who had loved him, trusted him, and thought he was actually a good guy were in a way also his victims.

To help ease my anguish, I filled my mind with thoughts of a beloved former pastor. While pastoring our church he was rearing his family with the help of his mother. His mentally ill wife was hospitalized for a number of years. This man would tell loving stories of their courtship and the early days of their marriage. His wife would come home for short visits and was lovingly cared for. He waited faithfully for years until she was released. She had recovered sufficiently to help in his ministry the rest of his life. Why couldn't every Christian be like that?

Disastrous marriages were hard to understand. The problem seemed so simple—just a case of lust and uncontrolled passion. Later I got a different insight.

More years passed. More infidelity disasters surfaced. Always incredible, and often involving someone I had confidence in. I finally got an inkling as to how it could happen.

I was now a young missionary in Burundi and was rather abruptly appointed head of the station. I was asked to participate in a church council. We sat with our backs to the wall on a cement bench that circled the inside of a rondavel. Board windows and a door opened to the sunshine, allowing us to see each other. Present were the national pastors, an African family, and another missionary. The discussion concerned a young man in his early teens, called home from a secondary school several hours' journey from us. He was confronted by a young girl who was pregnant with his child, but he refused to marry her. His reason? He wanted to continue his studies; he did not want to return home to be a husband and cultivator of corn and beans.

The scenario was this. For primary school he had been sent some distance from home to attend school on the mission station and stayed with relatives who lived nearer the school. At that time he was in his preteen years. He was given a place to sleep on the floor.

After some days, the mother said, "You are a relative. It is not right for you to sleep on the floor. You can sleep in the same bed as our young daughter."

That worked fine for a couple of years. As he entered his teen years, nobody said they should change the arrangement.

Now, early on in his secondary schooling, the family sent word: "Our daughter is pregnant. You will have to return and marry her." His reaction, "No way, I am going on to get an education."

At this point it was brought to the church council. Nothing in my training prepared me to enter into the decision. I was culturally out of it. No amount of discussion would change the young man's mind, even when told that he could not continue in school if he did not marry her. Finally, the wise senior pastor spoke, and I will never forget what was translated to me. Addressing the boy, he did not speak of adultery, but rather of stealing and dishonesty.

He said that in the story presented to us, "You did not steal anything. It was given to you. But to refuse to take responsibility for your own child is sin. Christianity that does not recognize sin is not Christianity."

His words gripped my mind. To that pastor, adultery was stealing. In this particular case the young man was not guilty of stealing or adultery. His guilt was for something else, even though it was still serious.

So all these distressing events and disappointments I had known in earlier years were not necessarily a result of lust and following unbridled passions. They were acts of dishonesty and stealing. They began in little acts of dishonesty in relationships that are not right. I began to understand the reason for moral failures. They were first of all acts of progressive dishonesty and then stealing. A man knows when he is being a bit too friendly; a woman knows when she is becoming emotionally dependent on someone other than her husband. This does not happen in an instant, with the devil saying, "Here is a chance to have an affair. Wouldn't it be exciting and fun?" But it starts with that nurse, that secretary, that boss or colleague, the one who is so much fun to be with, the person who starts being super thoughtful of you and worms his or her way into an emotional bond.

At this point an honest person says. "Whoops, too far! Cool it!" Or when tempting, provocative sights or situations present themselves, the person who won't steal will counter with, "Not mine"—and walk away. Despite our animal instincts, honest people will not steal that which is not theirs. How could someone be honest and betray the vows he has made to another? So with the scoring mentioned above, most adulterous situations would have to receive a score of twenty-four points. Twenty-four points off from our imaginary "Integrity Index" (nine for adultery, eight for stealing, and seven for lying), rather than a simple nine points for adultery.

He wills that I should holy be; that holiness I long to feel;
That full divine conformity to all my Savior's righteous will.

See, Lord, the travail of thy soul accomplished in the
change of mine;

And plunge me, every whit made whole; in all the depths of
love divine.

—Charles Wesley

Courage

Do not be afraid or terrified because of them,
for the Lord your God goes with you;
he will never leave you nor forsake you.
Deut. 31:6 NIV

In the culture I grew up in, the thinking was that to show fear was a terrible disgrace. I was actually more afraid of the guys thinking I might be afraid than I was of attempting something scary or risky. To be thought a sissy or coward was about the worst thing that could happen to a guy. Being the second among three boys added to the pressure. My dad contributed to this concept. His generation had a term: "softy." That was his word for "scaredy cat." He was number three of six boys in his family.

I read lots of stories about how Native American boys grew up in their culture. Young men were called braves. That was my ideal. When I turned thirteen, I vowed I would never again cry from pain, no matter how intense it became. But it was a façade; I was often trembling inside as I did things like dive off a thirty-foot diving tower to keep up with the other guys. My poor mother had grown up in a family of girls; she could not have imagined the things we attempted.

My sophomore year in high school I suffered a cracked ankle-bone while playing football. My cast was a badge of honor. My junior year, when I had made the varsity team, I limped proudly from bruises received in the previous Saturday night game.

But none of that was real courage. It was bravado. Sometimes, I envied girls who could say, "I am afraid." Men mask their fears. My surgeon friend, Charlie Robb, used to say, "God hates a coward." I never could find any scriptural basis for that statement, but it did tell me what he thought of showing fear.

The apostle Paul said, "When I am weak, then I am strong." Admitting how we feel is healthy and helps us own up to our fears. But most of us camouflage our inner feelings. We hope that this will not be the day others find us out. As long as we can keep it all bottled up, we appear to have it all together, and we feel safe. But that is not the mentality of a healthy mind.

Oswald Chambers, commenting on 1 Corinthians 10:31, wrote: "We mistake heroic actions for real heroes. It's one thing to go through a crisis grandly, yet quite another to go through every day glorifying God when there is no witness, no limelight, and no one paying even the remotest attention to us." [4]

Many things take courage and go almost unnoticed. My father often quoted the gospel song: "Dare to be a Daniel, dare to stand alone, Dare to have a purpose firm! Dare to make it known!" Of course his implied message was for us to have the courage to say no to tobacco and alcohol. Today, he would have added drugs to the list.

The Bible is full of other examples of courage. In the book of Esther, Queen Esther approached the king and interceded on behalf of the Jewish people, even though he could have had her killed for coming to him without being called. Her words were, "I will go to the king, even though it is against the law, and if I perish, I perish."

The Christian life requires courage to speak up in the face of dishonesty at work or injustice in our society. To remain silent on questions such as abortion is unconscionable, especially partial-birth abortion, which is just plain murder. For the church to not speak out loudly against this seems to me equal to the church remaining silent for so long about slavery prior to the Civil War.

It is hard to speak up. I admired a friend for speaking out in medical school. We were freshmen in psychiatry class. The lecturer made a statement seemingly condoning sexual immorality. My classmate raised his hand and asked in a strong voice, "Are you, sir, saying that this is normal and permissible?" The professor immediately backed down and stated that he did not mean to say what the student had thought. For a freshman, that took real courage.

To not speak up when your boss expects collaboration with dishonesty takes courage. I recall the story of a secretary who was about to be fired for not lying for her boss. She replied, "Well, you need to know that if I would lie for you, I would also lie to you." The boss changed his mind.

One area in which I often feel defeated is when a stranger, for instance a barber, asks me about my work.

I answer, "I worked as a missionary surgeon in Africa."

The comment always follows, "That must be very interesting."

My tendency is to reply, "Yes it is." Then the conversation changes.

I want to say, "Yes, it is interesting, but that is not why I do it."

When the next question arises, "Why do you do it?" I should reply, "Because I feel God wants me to do it."

Another area requiring courage for me was to get past my fear of failure. Prior to speaking in public, I often ask God, "Lord, is this the day I will fall flat on my face? You know I can't do this on my own." Then I concede to success or failure and leave the results to Him.

Failing was my biggest fear in medical school. Once I faced up to the possibility of failing and accepted the fact it was better to fail than not try, I began to have peace of mind. Similarly, when I finished my training as a general surgeon, I knew quite a few very capable surgeons who never bothered to take the American Board of Surgery certification examination. I think we all felt that our program was very good at training capable surgeons, but it did not have the high academic emphasis of the university programs. Some would say, "I am board eligible, but I did not bother to take the board exams." For my part, I just thought I was not smart enough. Eventually, thanks to the strong influence of a good friend, I began to study and take review courses to prepare for the boards. I tried the writtens and failed.

As I began to prepare for a second try, several board-certified friends, whom I admired as very capable doctors, confided in me,

"Well, I went up twice for the writtens and twice for the orals." I again decided it was better to try and fail than not to try at all. So, like these honest friends, I went up twice for the writtens and twice for the orals. It was a joy to eventually be certified by the American Board of Surgery. I became convinced that all those others who had not bothered to take the exams preferred to think they could make it than risk taking the examination and not make it

Being a missionary was another battle, requiring courage of another sort. Should we do this or should we not do this? We were bombarded with questions such as: "You're not going to take your children out there, are you? It might be all right to risk your life, but is it right to risk that of your children?" Other people were not the only ones saying that to me; my mind and fears were asking the same thing. After our first term, the African countries were becoming independent. Governments were often unstable, and the world situation more and more scary. Crises were everywhere. Hijacking planes became all too frequent. Today, it is terrorism, civil wars, AIDS, and on and on.

But how could I claim God's sufficiency, God's sovereignty, God's trustworthiness, and not put my life where my mouth is?

I once thought people without fears, doubts, or trembling were the ones who had courage—the cool, calm ones. I have come to realize those types are fortunate and rare, but they are not necessarily courageous. The courageous ones are those who are scared to death but go ahead in spite of their fears. And if it were true that God hates a coward, then there would be no hope for me.

One True, Invisible Church

Driving in Africa is an experience not easily described. It has to be suffered to be understood. Traveling from the western border of Rwanda to Kibogora mission, the last big bend in the bumpy clay road is marked by a life-size statue of the Virgin Mary. Beyond this statue appear a large Catholic church, one-story school buildings, and expanses of red clay. Whitewashed stone mark the footpaths. Sisal, palm, and eucalyptus trees shade the area, blocking further scrutiny, and here I sense a hint of "Private—Keep Out." Just past this point emerge glimpses of Lake Kivu and the distant Congo mountains. It can be restful in the early morning or nearing dusk, but during the day it is peppered with Rwandan children of all sizes. Schoolboys in shorts and shirts of khaki twill and girls in dark-blue, short-sleeve dresses dart from place to place—happy and busy with games that children devise when playground equipment is absent.

For some months I knew little of what lay behind that busy bend in the road.

By virtue of being the only doctor for miles around, I eventually became acquainted with the Catholic missionaries and the parish of Nyamasheke. Likewise, the Belgian sisters became acquainted with the Protestant parish and Kibogora Hospital. The missionaries of both these institutions believed they were serving the same risen Savior who died for our sins and commanded us to love one another, but both remained distant and mildly suspicious of each other. But mutual need brought mutual trust and respect, which eventually grew into a loving relationship.

The head of the Belgian and Rwandan sisters at Nyamasheke was the mother superior, Mère (Mother) Laurentine. For several years she seemed cold and distant when bringing students with medical needs. Though scarcely five feet tall, she had the bearing of a general. She was rather thin and trim, her black hair showed slightly from under her head covering, and, of course, she wore no makeup. A simple wedding band signified her marriage to the church. Like all the sisters in her order, she dressed in a gray uniform with the white head covering that trailed in back.

Patients came at any time it was convenient for them, which was confusing to our hospital schedule, so I set a special time for private consultations and asked those patients to come between 3 and 4 p.m., or any time if it was a true emergency. I explained that way, I would not be tied up in surgery or busy at other things. They in turn would not need to wait around and waste their time.

This arrangement went well for several months. Then one morning while making rounds in the wards I looked out the window, and there was Mère Laurentine and her next in command, Soeur Adrianne, standing on the veranda of our surgery building. They looked calm and composed but slightly impatient. Saying nothing to anyone, they just waited. I continued on my rounds, thinking, "They know I see private patients in the afternoon. They can just wait." I continued from bed to bed seeing patients, but I became uneasy since none of the ward patients presented an emergency. Finally, I thought, "I cannot be so impolite to the sisters. I might as well go up and see what they want."

I greeted them cordially with "Bonjour" and handshakes. Then I asked, "What brings you here this morning?"

Calmly, Soeur Adrianne responded, "Mère has been shot."

That got my attention! Slightly terrified, I escorted them into the surgery building, trying to appear calm as I sent for our missionary nurse. Not seeing any blood, and considering Mère's calm appearance, I could not believe it was as bad as it sounded. I had her sit on the x-ray table, trying to patiently stand aside as Miss Orcutt and Soeur Adrianne disrobed the patient. Somewhere in my medical experience I had learned that you don't just pull off the clothes of a Catholic sister, so I waited, wondering why there was no blood or holes in her habit. Finally, the chest was exposed, and there was a bleeding hole on her right thorax below the armpit about six ribs down. I listened to her chest. Breath sounds were normal. Heart sounds were normal. Her pulse was strong.

"We will take a chest x-ray," I told them.

The x-ray was normal. The lungs were inflated. No bullets or pieces of metal were in the chest or even in the soft tissue around the hole. I had her lie down, froze the area with local anesthetic, and probed the wound. Nothing there; I decided to excise the entire wound and path of the bullet. Carefully tracing the track of the bullet, I discovered that it ended without going into the chest cavity. Finding nothing, I cleansed the wound and sewed it up.

By that time their chauffeur had returned with another sister from Nyamasheke, bringing Mère's bloodstained undergarments. And inside was the bullet. I was confused and began to ask more questions. It seems that Catholic sisters are not only taught to always be calm, quiet, respectful, and never be in a hurry but also to always be clean. Perhaps in this case it was as the old saying goes, "Always wear clean underwear. You might get in an accident and be taken to the hospital."

What had happened that morning was this: Monsieur Claremont, a young Belgian professor who was living at Nyamasheke with his wife and baby, had seen a stray dog running around the schoolyard. Rabies was always a threat in our area, so Monsieur Claremont had gotten his rifle to handle the situation. He shot at—and missed— the dog, just as Mère Laurentine walked around the corner of the school building. The bullet had hit a rock, slowing it somewhat, and ricocheted up and hit mother superior in the side of the chest. Poor Monsieur Claremont remained behind, a near-basket case until he learned she was not near death. For me it remained one of my most amusing experiences in Africa.

That was the beginning of a long friendship between Louise and me and Mère Laurentine, who was the same age we were. Over the next twenty to thirty years the friendship and mutual respect grew.

Another experience occurred shortly after that when Soeur Monique, one of the Nyamasheke Rwandan sisters, entered our hospital with a bleeding peptic ulcer. She was young and repeatedly bled massively, requiring transfusions. The sisters wanted something to be done. In those days we did not have a gastroscope, but upper G-I x-rays from the capital Kigali confirmed the clinical diagnosis. I was hesitant to take on this case alone. But when Dr. David Crandall came to Kibogora, we decided to do it. We did a partial gastric resection, removing the lower end of the stomach, and cut the vagus nerve supply to the lower stomach. That cured Soeur Monique. Mère Laurentine was more grateful than when I had treated her gunshot wound.

When her superiors came from Belgium, she brought them to our house for tea. They expressed their great gratitude to the Kibogora staff. Each time Louise and I left for the U.S. we would receive a small gift and a note from Mère Laurentine praying that *le Seigneur* (the Lord) would bless and protect us on our trip. Whenever we talked, it became common to speak of the Lord.

Another experience clinched our understanding of the fellowship of Christ. One morning two other Nyamasheke sisters brought a newborn baby for me to examine. This child was clean, clothed in beautiful baby clothes—a little doll wrapped in a light yellow blanket. Someone near their dispensary had heard a baby's cries coming from the hole of an open-pit latrine. Calling for help from the dispensary, the rude toilet was carefully pulled apart, and the newborn baby was fished out. The abandoned baby girl was then taken to the dispensary, cleansed, and brought to the sisters. There, they had lovingly washed away every vestige of the feces and hurried to Kibogora Hospital. I could find nothing wrong with the baby, except that her eyes looked inflamed. So, I started antibiotic eye ointment and sent her back to the mission with orders for regular applications of the ointment. There she remained with the sisters who gave her the name "Rédempta," fittingly referring to the baby being redeemed, and I am sure, baptized.

I followed Rédempta's story with interest for some years. A member of Mère's family came from Belgium and adopted the baby. They changed her name to Elisabeth to remove all memory of the child's sad beginnings and reared her as their own. Her eyes eventually required corneal transplants, which were not entirely successful, but after several attempts she was able to see normally and go to school in Belgium.

The last two times Louise and I were in Rwanda we visited Mère Laurentine at Nyamasheke. She is now retired. Only one other Belgian sister remains with her. The entire mission is under national leadership. She is no longer mother superior but Sister Laurentine. When we saw her she greeted us warmly.

Wearing rubber boots, she came from a dairy barn with a big smile, saying, "You see, I am now a farmer."

In retirement she has fulfilled a longtime dream. Arranging transportation by airplane for five Holstein/Friesian calves, she began building her own dairy herd. Now, with the help of the local veterinarian, they are breeding these cows with local cows, raising the milk production above that of local herds. Sister Laurentine has a sparkling clean room where she processes the milk and produces milk products.

When asked if she planned to return to Belgium, she smiled and said, "I will die here."

We both laughed and agreed that it is just as close to heaven from Rwanda as it is from Belgium. It has not all been fun. Twice, she and the other Belgian sister have been robbed at gunpoint. That has not changed her determination to remain in Rwanda.

Having a Christian friend so different from us, yet with so many similar goals and essential beliefs, repeatedly brought to mind an experience from 1956. Our French teacher in Belgium, Professor Van Dyke, took us on several excursions to visit points of interest in Antwerp. He was an excellent professor and very interested in seeing us succeed as missionaries in the then-Belgian Congo. One of the places we visited was the ancient cathedral in Antwerp. After showing us around the beautiful building, explaining the windows, art, and images—so serene and beautiful, and so different from the plain little church I had grown up in—he said, "Now just pause, remain silent, meditate, and think about God and His intentions for His Church. Could He ever have willed or envisioned the fragmentation of His Church that has taken place down through history?"

He did not ask for an answer, and we, mostly Protestants, remained silent.

One of my Sunday school teachers used to say, "There will be far more Catholics in heaven than Free Methodists." Of course we all had to agree. That being the case, should we not practice fellow-shipping here on earth as we will in heaven, remembering that Christ prayed for us that we might be one? For some years now, I have had "The Sisters" on my prayer list.

Medical Missions—A Specialty?

(The following is adapted from a talk to the Spring Arbor University Science Faculty.)

A medical colleague, Dr. David Stewart, missionary at a neighboring mission hospital in Burundi, insisted that medical missions should be considered a specialty all its own. I resisted that concept for many years but finally decided it is true.

There are many things on the mission field that I learned from more experienced missionary doctors. There were many things I learned on my own by trial and error. In the army we were taught to use our Yankee ingenuity. That meant if you don't have what you need, don't be blocked; think up an alternative way.

Experience is the best teacher, but often a cruel teacher. Experiences that have no precedent are forever ambushing you. Like on one sleepy Sunday afternoon at Kibogora, when some men showed up at our builder's house to borrow a rope to get three men out of a toilet hole. Someone had dropped a new Bic pen down the hole while at a wedding reception. Three men, a bit tipsy from too much banana beer, had said, "No problem, we can get it out for you." The next part of the story, I can only imagine. I got involved when they brought two in for medical treatment. The toilet hole was perhaps twenty feet deep. One victim was on a stretcher, almost unconscious, the other able to walk, and a third one left behind, dead.

So for you scientists, what toxins would be in a toilet hole? Would it be sewer gas? I suppose skatole, methane, and perhaps hydrogen sulfide. My problem was to treat two stuporous men. We first addressed the patient on the stretcher—out of his mind and covered with slimy, wet fecal matter. Probably from being a surgeon, the only place I thought we could protect ourselves and attend to him was in our operating room. We dressed in protective clothing of caps, masks and gowns, and rubber gloves. We had his buddies strip him naked for us, but at this point, being intoxicated from alcohol and sewer gases, he became maniacal and swung wildly at us, and became completely unmanageable.

We grasped his arm, and as we began to struggle we almost lost our balance on the waxed floor, now super slippery with smeared feces. I envisioned two of us and the patient all piled up on the floor. Eventually, we subdued him, cleaned him up, and examined him before admitting him to the hospital for observation. He and the other man recovered uneventfully. The body of the third one was brought in for a medical legal exam to determine the cause of death. I agreed to this on the condition that he be brought in washed and cleanly dressed for burial. Medical school never prepared me for anything like that.

I learned that a doctor can often learn something from a good nurse. In my surgical training I had rotated through the neurosurgical service, but in Africa, I often had to be the neurosurgeon. One time, two night watchmen from a European's coffee plantation were brought to our hospital. Both had their skulls bashed in with a hammer while they slept. Both were unconscious. While I was working on one's wounds, picking out fragments of bone and trying to figure out what I should pull out and what would be better left in place, I lifted out a large piece from his supraorbital ridge (the bone just under your eyebrow). I stood there asking myself, "Will it heal if I stick it back in, or will it die and necrose from lack of blood supply?" At this moment my missionary nurse said, "I knew a man back home who was missing one of those." "Really?" I asked, and tossed the piece in the pan with the other bone fragments.

Another time, I went to see one of the consultations the medical assistant had reserved for me. It was almost noon. The man was sitting in the waiting room with a knit cap on, awake and talking. He had been hit with an ax or machete a few days earlier. I lifted off his hat, and there was his brain open to the outdoors, pulsating with each beat of the heart. What to do with a dirty wound and a skull opened for a couple of days already? Dale Nitzsche, nurse anesthetist, told me of a case in North Dakota in which a man came in with his skull opened from a manure shovel.

"What did the neurosurgeon do?" I asked.

"He just packed it open with iodoform gauze for a few days to clean up the wound," I was told.

"Okay, let's do that." That gave me time to read up on it, start antibiotics, and close the skull wound a few days later.

I had very little training in radiology other than learning to read x-rays. In the U.S. the technicians did all the mechanical things. So it was with a lot of ignorance I started doing my own x-rays. When a German electrician from a nearby tea plantation hooked up our donated 100 MA x-ray machine, I began experimenting. I wore a lead apron and lead gloves, so I felt comfortable about myself, but how was I to know whether I was overexposing the patient to radiation? I had tables that gave me some idea of how many MA seconds I should use. To experiment I put a bunch of tools from the garage on the table and shot an x-ray of them. The film looked fine. Next, I borrowed Columbus, one of the missionaries' cats, put him in a gunnysack, and shot a film of him. His entire skeleton looked fine on the developed film. Columbus was very happy to get out of the gunnysack and never sought medical care after that. I got a little braver and started taking x-rays of extremities only. They were good. Eventually, I got brave enough to shoot x-rays of chests, skulls, and abdomens. All went okay, so I trained an African nurse to be my technician, taking and developing films.

After a while I began to worry about my staff, who worked in the room adjoining the x-ray room. Was it possible that over time they were building up radiation exposure? I went to Kigali and explained my concerns to the Belgian radiologist. He reassured me by saying that a thirty-centimeter brick wall was just as effective as a lead shield. Since our walls were one and one-half bricks thick, or thirty centimeters, he felt we were in no danger, but to be sure he gave me a couple of mammogram films that were packed in cardboard enve-lopes. I was told to tape the film on the side of the wall where our staff worked, leave them there for a month, then develop them. If radiation was coming through the walls, the films would turn black; if no rays were coming through, the films would be transparent when developed. If gray, that would indicate a slight amount was getting through. When the month was past, I developed the mammogram films and was delighted to find them clear, showing that no radiation was penetrating our walls to where the ladies worked preparing the surgical packs each day.

One of our biggest challenges came with cholera epidemics. Cholera is a disease that strikes with sudden onset of watery diarrhea, the so-called "rice-water stools." The secret is to keep up with the fluid loss for a few days until the body can handle the infection. It was necessary to keep the patients on a cot with a bedpan handy, or even put the bedpan on the floor under the patient's buttocks with an opening allowing the gushes of diarrhea to pour into the bedpan. If we could keep up with the fluids for a couple of days, they lived. If we could not, they died. But we could not distill water fast enough. Rainwater is a good substitute, but removing the gross dirt and contamination is difficult. In desperation I resorted to sterilizing filtered spring water from the valley. We made normal saline with nine grams of sodium chloride per liter, and 5 percent glucose with fifty grams of glucose per liter. Our nurses would check on them every hour or two, day and night. If their pulse was above one hundred beats per minute, they speeded up the intravenous; if below one hundred they slowed the IV. It became rare to lose a patient after that.

Research. Is it possible in a mission hospital? It is not only possible, but also it is desirable. Dr. Dennis Burkitt, a British surgeon, first described a lymphoma of the jaw, now known as Burkitt's lymphoma. He mapped out whole regions of Africa and made the association between altitude and mosquito habitations to suggest that the malignant tumor was caused by insect bites. He also studied the amount of fiber in Africans' diets as compared to the European diet, thus associating fiber with a low incidence of colon cancer.

My first term, I reported the high incidence of peptic ulcer of the duodenum that we were finding in Burundi and reported it to the *Archives of Surgery* journal. To my amazement, it not only got published but also received editorial comment on the geographical distribution of disease by one of the leading peptic ulcer authorities from the University of Florida. It appeared in *Archives of Surgery* in August 1963.

About two years ago, one of our African physicians did research on a number of peptic ulcer cases and tested gastroscopy biopsies for the bacterium Helicobacter pylori. He found that 90 percent of our ulcer cases were positive for Helicobacter pylori. That was in line with present findings in the developed world and is the reason for treating peptic ulcers with antibiotics added to acid blockers and antacids at present. Today it is rare in the U.S. to even operate on peptic ulcer patients. In Africa we still see so many of the complications of peptic ulcer that operating on these is a large part of our surgical load.

At Kibogora we live on the edge of beautiful Lave Kivu, about sixty miles long and twenty to thirty miles wide. Swimming is one of the fun things that our missionary kids do. When I first came to Kibogora, I was told that Schistosomiasis did not exist in Lake Kivu. But eventually, one of our missionary nurses contracted an infection with S. mansoni, the intestinal form. That is transmitted by human feces to water and to snails and back to people via the cercaria from the snails in the lake that enter through a swimmer's skin. (It is similar to "swimmer's itch," but that goes no deeper than the skin). How was I to find out if where we were swimming was safe? Did our missionary get it from wading through a creek or swamp somewhere?

I went to our laboratory techs and showed them a picture of a Schistosome mansoni egg and promised them one hundred francs for each one they could show me in the next two weeks. Within a few days, I had to start paying up. Sadly, I learned that we did have Schistosome mansoni in our area. But where? We went with our motor launch to the islands and peninsulas and announced we were testing for worms; any we found we would treat for free. We had loads of customers and soon found what areas were the most highly infested.

One Belgian medical authority offered to give me guinea pigs to put in a cage with their hind legs submerged. That sounded complicated and cruel. I thought of a better way. Our secondary school, students lived in a dorm near the lake and bathed in the lake. Thus they were exposed almost daily during three years of school. Using students was much better than guinea pigs. After all, we were concerned about people—not guinea pigs.

I had learned it could be assuredly diagnosed by a biopsy of rectal mucosa. I devised a technique, working through an anoscope, of tearing off several snips of rectal mucosa with a surgical instrument known as a Judd-Allis forceps. We talked the senior boys into having rectal biopsies. I told them how terrible it would be to leave school with this infection. Their whole life could be ruined. But if they would submit to a rectal biopsy, we would treat them free plus treating any other worms we found. They all signed up. (Someone said I should have been an evangelist.) We then mounted the biopsies in saline between glass slides and looked at them with the microscope using the high-power objective. Out of sixty-six boys we found three positive cases. But these three positive cases came from home provinces that bordered on Lake Kivu. Maybe they did not even get infected at Kibogora. I began to breathe easier, and we began to swim again in Lake Kivu. The next year we repeated the exams and found again the exact same results—sixty-six students biopsied, with three positive for S. mansoni.

As the years passed, a few more missionaries became infected, but by then the treatment had become very simple and cheap. The treatment was not dangerous, with several new antischistomiasis medications. So we all began to swim again.

These are just some of the things I enjoy talking about in missionary medicine. If I were to tell you about my blunders and all the dumb things I did, it would take much more space.

In hindsight, it has been a wonderful life for me and for our family. I think I speak for the entire family when I say there have been no regrets in leading the type of life we have had on the mission field.

Providence

Trust in the Lord with all your heart,
and lean not to your own understanding;
in all your ways acknowledge Him,
and He shall direct your paths.
Proverbs 3:5-6

In early 1945, I, an eighteen-year-old, was being trained as an infantry rifleman. One of my close friends had just been killed in the Battle of the Bulge. Halfway through training it was announced there would be an examination given for returning to college. I had already taken six months of college in the Army Special Training Program. It was intensive, covering one year of college in six months—a pre-engineering program heavy with math, physics, and chemistry, and definitely not my thing. I passed and got a year of college credit, but I did not excel. Regarding the possibility of continuing college after basic training, my records read, "Eligible, but not recommended." I took the exam. At the end, I was called in for an interview with an officer who told me they would recommend my return to college, but I had to sign an application. I squirmed a bit and finally said, "I don't really want to go." The lieutenant, a really nice guy, looked at me with compassion and started to plead with me as though he were my dad or big brother. Finally, I said, "Okay, put me down. I'll go if the opportunity comes." But the opportunity never came.

Enticements were offered to train in the paratroops for the airborne infantry. I did not want that, but then came the chance to apply for the ski troops for mountain fighting in Europe. Another Michigander, Richard Snyder (no relation), and I applied. We heard nothing from this, but when the orders came for our company to ship out to the East Coast, we two were left behind at Camp Robinson. Oh joy, we were headed for ski troops, we reasoned. But that was one of the ironies of the army; when our orders came, Big Snyder, as Richard was nicknamed, and Little Snyder (because I was smaller) received orders to report to Fort Ord, California, obviously for duty in the Pacific Theater. Great! The war ends in Europe, and all our buddies we started out with got shipped east for Europe, and two stupid Snyders head for war in the Pacific. Unfortunately, we had not yet learned the army axiom, "Never volunteer for anything."

Romans 8:28 in the New English Bible says that in everything God "cooperates" for good. To me, that indicates that God may not have planned the results, but He can turn them into good eventually.

Our troopship was small and cramped with five thousand soldiers. No one had much space to himself. None of us knew our destination. But, as our twenty-four day journey progressed, the weather became increasingly hotter. We wondered why we had been issued heavy winter clothing, including long-legged underwear. Eventually, we pulled into a harbor and for the first time were told where we were—the Marshall Islands. The next day we left in a convoy of ships, escorted by naval destroyers. We now had entered dangerous waters frequented by enemy submarines. Tired of looking only at the Pacific Ocean and the horizon, I was fascinated by the destroyers purring along beside us. I enjoyed the sight and was not particularly fearful. I had passed that stage one night back at Ford Ord. Separated from my colleagues of the first year, on an upper bunk, and feeling alone in the dark, I was suddenly seized by fear. We had just gone through two weeks of firing and reviewing all our weapons: rifles, machine guns, bazookas, and hand grenades. I thought of my home-town friends who had already been killed and reasoned, "Probably each family will lose one, and I will be the one for our family." Panic gripped me. Eventually, these words came to me: "Lo, I am with you always, even to the end of the earth." The quote was not quite correct, but that's what came to me, and tears overwhelmed me. My fear lifted, never again to return in the months ahead.

On shipboard time passed slowly. At night the doors and windows were totally blacked out; the sleeping areas were hot and stuffy. Bunks were like shelves, and I chose the top one, the fifth row up. Our next stop was the Caroline Islands, where the convoy broke up and we traveled alone again. The last night of our voyage we wound in and out of numerous small islands, part of the Philippines. The sea, now serene, was illuminated by an enormous full moon, its beams glimmering across the water. I stood at the rail in awe, looking at silhouettes of various small islands. In the morning we pulled into Manila Bay.

South of Manila at the 29th Replacement Depot, our winter clothes were turned in for light tropical wear. The troop buildup around Manila was around one million. Fighting was still going on in northern Luzon; invasion of Japan was next. Camp construction was incomplete. Toilets were primitive, showers nonexistent. The July heat was oppressive, and we were feeling the need of showers when a tropical downpour moved in. We stripped off our clothes, grabbed a bar of soap, and lathered up. Just about that time, the cloud passed on, leaving us covered with suds. In desperation, we ran to the trees, shaking branches to rinse with the water from the leaves. A strange sight in this all-men's world—jaybird naked, swinging from tree branches like a bunch of monkeys.

A few days later we were moved to the Fifth Replacement Depot, a highly organized tent city with proper chapels, post-exchange dining halls, and even electricity and running water. Here we were processed for our stay in the Philippines. On August 9, 1945, while I was on guard duty patrolling an area around the post office, the blaring music on the post office radio was suddenly interrupted by a news bulletin. The second atomic bomb had been dropped on the Japanese city of Nagasaki, and the Japanese would surrender on condition they could keep Emperor Hirohito in power. A wild excitement erupted in the camp; some guards shot off their rifles in celebration. For me it was a moment of great jubilation. "Yippee! We're going home!" Or so I thought. It had not occurred to me that it might be a bit complicated; there were at least a million other GIs ahead of me, those who had fought their way up from New Guinea and the southern Philippine Islands. These were older-looking soldiers, with leathery, tanned skin now yellow from years of taking Atebrine for malaria prevention. A point system was established, giving points for each month overseas and perhaps a few other considerations, like whether they were single or married, fathers with children, wounded or never wounded. I remember that my points added up to seven, while many had numbers in the forties, fifties, or sixties. So we "kids" resigned ourselves to a long stay in the Philippines. My turn did not come up until over a year later, when my points finally made me eligible to go home.

Within a few more weeks I was assigned to the 743rd Artillery Gun Battalion. I said goodbye to the only buddy who had come into the army with me from Michigan, back in July 1944. We were nothing alike and had very little in common, but I shook hands, choking back tears and a lump in my throat. No one else had I known for more than a few weeks. Richard Snyder and I had been together from day one.

God moves in mysterious ways. How could I have been rolled down the chute like an apple in a sorting machine and been completely separated from everyone I knew? I climbed onto the big truck bed of a military vehicle and ended up in the little town of Paranaque on the outskirts of Manila. We enlisted men were assigned as permanent personnel, staffing a new replacement depot. This camp was for processing officers, nurses, and WACs, arriving or returning to the U.S.

I was a lone Yankee in a passel of southerners. Initially, I was put on all kinds of jobs. I was afraid I would end up as a "general flunky," doing dirty jobs that needed to be done, but after one of these details I was offered the job of "striker" (or orderly) for the commandant, Colonel Bean. As his orderly I had a pretty good deal. No one dared bother me now. Wherever I went or whatever I did, no one knew whether I was on a personal mission for the colonel or what I was up to. All I had to do was tend to his quarters, send his laundry out, and run a few errands now and then. Besides this, the colonel paid me extra for my work. My time was my own, and I was free to attend all the events at the chapel—services, Bible studies, and so forth.

A couple of months later I got another job. The supply officer needed a typist. The personnel officer said to me, "This may get me in big trouble with the CO, but I am assigning you to be a clerk-typist in the supply office." My rank got boosted to corporal. I was also happier, because there was a certain contempt for anyone who was a shoe-shiner for the commanding officer.

A few months later the chaplain needed an assistant; he asked the CO if he could have Snyder for his chaplain's assistant. Since the CO knew me personally, he agreed. As chaplain's assistant I had my own sleeping room in the back of the chapel, chauffeured the chaplain around in his Jeep, did his typing, made out the bulletin for Sunday, and generally buddied around with him.

When I had left home to enter the army's active reserve I feared greatly all the temptations ahead. I was on my own, scarcely stabilized from the bombardments of oscillating emotions and lusts characterizing my early teen years. Fortunately, I had learned something about faith and trust. My first night in the army, and to the end of my army career, I knelt briefly at my bedside in prayer. I reasoned that if I deny Jesus before men, He might deny me later. Looking back, I often wonder if this was pharisaical. But it was a declaration to others that I was a different sort of guy, maybe weird, but marching to a different drummer. For me, it seemed right. It also obligated me to act like a Christian.

As chaplain's assistant I was permanently marked. Living in the chapel was easier than being in a tent with seven other guys, only one of which, besides me, did not regularly visit the prostitutes available everywhere. Working for the chaplain I became acquainted with other Christian GIs around the country. I began to attend the GI gospel hour every Saturday night in Manila. Often unsaved buddies went along. Missionaries who had been interned by the Japanese were now free and eager to get all the help they could from servicemen. Opportunities abounded to work with small Protestant churches, which were struggling to recover from the long Japanese occupation. One night, as I was walking alone, praying, and looking up into the night sky, I felt overwhelmed with a desire to come back to the Philippines as a missionary. And the best part of this was a sense that God would be pleased and had indeed called me to this purpose. All that had transpired in my army time made perfect sense. I no longer had any questions as to how I could get separated from everyone I had come into the army with and end up at this camp alone, except for God's presence.

God's providence continues to amaze me. As I look back over the years, it is not unlike certain high points in the mountains of Rwanda where one can look back and see distant dirt roads winding through the valleys, across narrow dangerous bridges, over swirling streams; roads winding round and round and up the mountain, along narrow cliffs where the road cuts through the side of a hill with a high cliff wall on one side and nothing but a long drop to the valley on the other. I would warn the uninitiated of the dangers, the things they should know—like "Don't go through this way in the rainy season" or "Don't drive there at night. Always make sure you have a full tank of fuel, and food and water along. Never travel alone. Always take a national with you."

In Africa, I learned that when the road forks, if I studied it a bit, I could see which was the road most traveled. Almost always this was the way to go. The other continued to narrow down, eventually showing two worn tire tracks; finally it ended in a footpath—going nowhere. In life, I have found the opposite.

In my life I can see some very dangerous forks in the road. Some were where I made the right decision and did not even know it was crucial until I looked back. Other times I made the wrong decision, but somehow God in His providence brought me back on track. He seemed to know when I truly wanted His guidance but unwittingly took the wrong path. God also knows when we know very well which way to go but choose the easiest, most pleasant road.

I remember a critical point in our lives. I had looked toward the mission field from my days in the Philippine Islands. Now that I was a doctor, our board asked us to go to India and appointed us to go there after one year of surgical training. As the time drew near I listened to those who urged me to finish my surgical training. They spoke of the tumultuous world situation, how irrational it was to take our young children overseas. "Stay put, get all the training you can get. Let the world settle down," we were advised. At this juncture I was in great inner turmoil. The joy went out of my life as

I decided to postpone going. I knew that in the Christian world you need to take the road less traveled, and here I was looking down another road. It was bright and sunny and attractive, but I was not at peace taking it.

I made plans to leave the residency, pack our things, and be on our way. But the appointment to India bothered us a great deal. We were advised that we would have to send our children fifteen hundred miles away to boarding school. That we could not face, nor did we feel God was asking us to do that. At the same time there were needs in Africa. I took off a few days from work, and we drove to Sault St. Marie (The Soo) to talk to furloughing missionary nurse Margaret Holton. We arrived on Sunday night and got a motel room, and she came over with her slides and stories of the needs in Rwanda and Burundi. In that room, with our kids falling asleep, we sat up and talked. Margaret insisted the need was tremendous, and we should consider going there.

Before going to see Margaret, I had called the mission board and told them if they could find someone else who did not feel as we did about India, we would prefer to go to Africa. A classmate from college and I were to meet with them on Tuesday morning at Winona Lake. I wanted to meet this classmate before we both talked to the board. I wanted to tell him of my reservations about India and let him know that I did not want him to consider it if he felt the way we did. We left The Soo early Monday morning to be at Winona Monday night. But as we got into Lower Michigan we heard of a bad snowstorm in the Grand Rapids area, so I cut west to miss it. It only got worse, so I cut back east toward Kalamazoo thinking we would go straight south on Route 131. Cars were going into the ditch, and the roads were becoming impassable. Visibility was terrible. We made it into Kalamazoo and got a hotel room. Cars were pulling off the roads.

The next morning the March storm was over, the sun was out, and the roads were clear as we started for Winona. But we could not make it before early afternoon. I learned my former classmate, also a doctor, had been there, readily accepted the appointment to India, and left. My appointment was changed to Africa with almost no discussion. Did God send the snowstorm?

India did not grant a visa for a missionary doctor. This colleague finally decided God meant him to practice in the States, while we spent most of my professional career in Africa. I never felt I had manipulated that situation, nor did he. I count it as God's providence.

In my life, I tried to follow the road I thought right, and when I did not, I made some painful detours. But God has a way of steering you back onto the right path. Often, I did not know, until looking back, that it was the right one, but God did.

I love this portion of Robert Frost's poem "The Road Not Taken":

> I shall be telling this with a sigh
> Somewhere ages and ages hence.
> Two roads diverged in a wood, and I—
> I took the one less traveled by,
> And that has made all the difference. [5]

Neighbors in the Global Village

The days were hot, the roads dusty, and our Toyota Land Cruiser's nickname was the "Bone Crusher." Eight hours of being pummeled tested the endurance of both my passenger and me. Suddenly coming into an area of road construction, my companion, Bishop Aaron, looked at the heavy machinery and remarked, "Follow the bulldozer! That is what we learned in our recent conference on church growth." In spreading the gospel as fast as possible we should "follow the bulldozer." To him the idea seemed to be sound and right on track. It would mean going where the population was growing fastest.

I never forgot that advice and reflected on it a lot. I was impressed that it seemed sound, but in many ways it bothered me. In fact, many church-growth concepts worry me. I am concerned that the numbers emphasis has reached our overseas church. Numbers had never been important in Africa. People were always there by the thousands. The problem always had been in finding ways to disciple them and ground them in the faith. I hated to see our pastors get caught up in the numbers game of the West. It was important to them only as they saw how it excited our people in the mother church.

Incidentally, I could never forget the time Pastor Bararu was escorting his father home to die. His inoperable cancer was not helped by the long trip to Kibogora Hospital. A hired taxi leaving Cyangugu pulled in behind a large road grader; the machinery was suddenly put into reverse and backed over the little taxi, abruptly ending the life of Bararu's father. Mournfully, Bararu brought his father's body back to Kibogora for a funeral. No compensation, no investigation, just another case of a bad, bad day in the Third World. Lesson? It is not always best to "follow the bulldozer" too closely.

And as a mission strategy, is it really the best advice to follow the bulldozer? If we did, many would be left behind—the weak, the lame, the blind, the deaf, the sick, the injured. Are we in it for the numbers? Is our philosophy like that of big business? Must we go where the money is—that is, where the results are the most noticeable?

Primary health programs and preventive medicine programs have had a similar philosophy; since it costs too much to run hospitals, do major surgery, x-rays, laboratory studies, and all that, it is in the best interests of the masses to prevent disease. After all, everyone knows that an ounce of prevention is worth a pound of cure. But here again, we minister only to those who can go with the bulldozer; we leave the weak, the injured, sick, lame, deaf, and blind behind. With prevention we minister primarily to the healthy and the strong to keep them healthy and strong. Did Jesus do that?

In Matthew 8:16-17 it is written: "When evening came, many who were demon-possessed were brought to him, and he drove out the spirits with a word and healed all the sick. This was to fulfill what was spoken through the prophet Isaiah: 'He took up our infirmities and carried our diseases'" (NIV).

In Matthew 11:2-5, when John the Baptist was discouraged, in prison, and soon to be beheaded, he sent his disciples to Jesus and asked, "Are you the one who was to come, or should we expect someone else?" Jesus simply answers, "Go back and report to John what you hear and see: The blind receive sight, the lame walk, those who have leprosy are cured, the deaf hear and the good news is preached to the poor" (NIV).

The inescapable conclusion seems that both Isaiah and Jesus are on record that the hallmark of "true religion" is the compassion that goes with the gospel. Toward the end of the last century, who was one of the most respected Christians in the entire world? Every time I ask this, Mother Teresa's name comes up. She spoke with power. The world listened. Who could forget the picture of little Mother

Teresa at the Presidential Prayer Breakfast? Standing on a box to reach the podium, she told the world what she thought about abortion. As those present stood and gave her an ovation, the President and Vice-President conspicuously remained seated, nervously moving their drinking glasses back and forth in front of them. What were her credentials? Good works—the relief of suffering of the neglected and dying. Nothing else!

The apostle James, Jesus' own half-brother, tells us to show our faith by our deeds and asks how we can see a brother in need and do nothing about it. He seems to ask, "What good is your faith anyhow if that is the way you are?" (James 2:14-17, paraphrased).

And back to Jesus' words again, where He speaks of separating the sheep and goats. He speaks of Himself as having been sick, hungry, and in prison. His words make me shudder: "The king will reply, 'I tell you the truth, whatever you did for one of the least of these brothers of mine, you did for me.' Then he will say to those on his left, 'Depart from me, you who are cursed; into the eternal fire prepared for the devil and his angels. For I was hungry and you gave me nothing to eat, I was thirsty, and you gave me nothing to drink, I was a stranger and you did not invite me in, I needed clothes and you did not clothe me. I was sick and in prison and you did not look after me'" (Matt. 25:40-43 NIV).

I hope we never hear, "Depart from me; I do not know you."

And what about the Wesleys and their social programs in the eighteenth century? Also, in our own country, what religious group is the most respected by the unbelieving world? It seems to me that the Salvation Army is that group. They speak by their actions to an unbelieving world. They follow in the tradition of the Wesleys.

Can we have faith without works? Or can we do preventive medicine without curative medicine? Can a woman with a ruptured uterus find comfort in an immunization? In medicine it is now realized that you can't run a health program without both prevention and cure. Likewise, can we run programs of evangelism and missions without humanitarian services? Does God still own the cattle on a thousand hills? Or has He told us to trim our programs to the most economical, practical, and expedient? I think He has shown us the pattern to follow in His Word. He will provide if we follow His example. Following the bulldozer might give us big numbers and a heady sense of really changing the world, but does it follow the pattern set by Jesus?

Do medical missions play a role in evangelization? Many times Bishop Aaron told me that before Kibogora Hospital was in full function the Free Methodist Church endured a great deal of opposition from the dominant Catholic Church of our area. We were ignored at best, and at worst we were looked down upon and actively opposed. However, with the coming of the hospital the Catholic priests and sisters began to come for medical care. We gave them professional courtesy, treating them kindly without charge. They brought serious medical cases from their schools; our doctors and nurses treated sisters and priests who suffered major illnesses and injuries. The opposition, in face of these acts of kindness, evaporated, and since then we have enjoyed respect and cooperation from the Catholic mission.

Do medical missions play a role in evangelization? After the evacuation of 1994 and the ethnic war it looked as though we were finished working in Rwanda. The missionaries and most of the national church leadership had evacuated. The Free Methodist Church at that time was estimated to have a membership of forty thousand. However, through the avenue of relief agencies and NGOs, our medical missionaries were able to return. They were first to establish contact with our church in Rwanda and have remained there. Through great danger and risk to their lives, they were able to let the national church know they had not been abandoned. Since the war, our medical mission in Rwanda has supported the church and helped it during the subsequent period of uncertainty. Now the church is estimated to have a membership of ninety thousand. It has reorganized and is functioning admirably. God found a way to continue building His church, and medical missions played a major role in all this.

Finally, how do we react to the oft-quoted statement that more people pass through the hospitals of the world than the churches of the world? Aren't hospitals areas of evangelism too? When young doctors and nurses come saying, "God is calling me to work with the have-nots of the world," what do mission agencies say to them? And what about the Parable of the Good Samaritan? Are we as a church going to pass by on the other side of the road and leave the bruised and dying to go without care? Who are our neighbors in today's global village?

Jesus told us who our neighbors are by telling a story. "'There was once a man traveling from Jerusalem to Jericho. On the way he was attacked by robbers. They took his clothes, beat him up, and went off leaving him half-dead. Luckily, a priest was on his way down the same road, but when he saw him he angled across to the other side. Then a Levite religious man showed up; he also avoided the injured man.

"'A Samaritan traveling the road came on him. When he saw the man's condition, his heart went out to him. He gave him first aid, disinfecting and bandaging his wounds. Then he lifted him onto his donkey, led him to an inn, and made him comfortable. In the morning he took out two silver coins and gave them to the innkeeper, saying 'Take good care of him. If it costs any more, put it on my bill—I'll pay you on my way back.'

"'What do think? Which of the three became neighbor to the man attacked by robbers?

"'The one who treated him kindly,' the religion scholar responded.

"Jesus said, 'Go and do the same'" (Luke 10:29-37 Message).

When Will We Be Home?

You are no longer foreigners and aliens,
but fellow citizens with God's people
and members of God's household.
Eph. 2:19 NIV

"Cabin crew, prepare for takeoff." What sweet words to the ears of someone headed home. Being a foreigner is exciting for a while, but not to be an alien is much better. It is being home, a citizen, "one of us," *chez nous* in French. One time as we crossed the last river into our home Prefecture of Cyangugu, Rwanda, our national pastor remarked that we were home, "where nobody can grab us." He meant where they won't apprehend us, lock us up, or accuse us of something.

Coming into the U.S. we walk boldly up to a line beneath the sign, "United States citizens, and holders of Green Cards." What a comfort! One of our American pastors wrote an account of his travels in Africa— the exciting events, the scary things, the muddy, slippery roads, the beautiful things, but we were amused by his closing words: "God bless America!" We knew exactly what he was expressing.

A citizen, not an alien, demands his rights. When the Belgian Congo became independent in the sixties, *Time* magazine carried an account of a Jeep-load of the local military crashing through an intersection without hesitating and shouting to those arriving from another direction, "Attention, pour les citoyens!" (Get out of the way of the citizens). I remember driving up to an isolated border post in Burundi. I failed to stop the car exactly at the stop sign. An angry border functionary came to the door of the immigration hut and shouted for me to back my car up to exactly where the sign was.

He shouted, "Can't you read? Don't you have any brains?"

"Oui, monsieur, je m'excuse," I replied.

He was home; I wasn't. He was a citizen, I an alien. Such indignities! They make my stomach churn and my blood boil, but still I realize I am not home. I am a visitor, a stranger, a foreigner, an alien. But on a plane heading home, I sit back, fasten my seatbelt while someone of my own race, in my own language, and perhaps of my own faith says, "Cabin crew, prepare for takeoff." I watch people who look like me hustle about putting door handles into the locked position. As the plane taxies out, I breathe a sigh of relief. My blood pressure drifts down. And I begin to think there is really no place like home, "where nobody can grab us!"

The Man Without a Country was written by Edward Hale to inspire patriotism at the time of the Civil War. I read it as a schoolboy and was pained with the thought of someone renouncing his own country, never to find a home after that—never being able to say, "How good it is to be home."

I have close friends who are refugees—people I have lived and worked with. They are doctors, teachers, pastors—people I know and love. These people have no hope of going home. Some have nightmares of people stalking them. Some are terrified that a stranger is inquiring about them. Some fear they will be deported, but deported to where? Will all of the family be deported? Or only one member?

"Where are my friends when I need them?" they ask. "If only I had a scholarship, I could stay here as a student. If only I had a profession, they would let me stay. If I only had a valuable skill. If only…if only…if only."

So the letters come from friends without a country; from South Africa, Kenya, Tanzania, Congo, Ivory Coast, Benin, Belgium, Scotland, Norway, Canada, the U.S. "Dear Parent," they begin. "Greetings in Jesus' name."

Just Do It

The path of the righteous is like
the first gleam of dawn,
shining ever brighter till the full light of day.
But the way of the wicked is like deep darkness;
they do not know what makes them stumble...
Let your eyes look straight ahead,
fix your gaze directly before you.
Consider the paths for your feet and
take only ways that are firm.
Do not swerve to the right or the left;
keep your foot from evil.
Proverbs 4:18-9, 25-27

It is interesting how families have little in-house jokes or sayings. One at our house comes from the words of our third son when he was eight years old. The setting was at Big Twin Lake in northern Michigan. All the adults and older kids had taken their turn at water-skiing. Now it would be Steve's skiing debut. He turned to me and said, "I might as well gather up my guts and try it." Interpretation: "It will take a lot of guts, but I guess I might as well try." It is tough being a boy. Girls can say, "No, I am too scared." But boys, especially with brothers and male cousins, can't get off so easily. Steve later became the outstanding skier in our family.

Hard things in our family are often approached with the comment, "I guess I will gather up my guts and do it." Lots of things are not easy, but often you have to just do it. One of my missionary colleagues used to say, "You'll never do it any younger." That was his way of referring to putting things off or procrastinating.

Earlier in my life, when I began doing surgery on my own, I had scheduled a difficult case, and I was tempted to postpone the operation. In the halls I met a colleague in whom I had a lot of confidence. I laid out my reason for hesitating. He listened carefully, then replied, "If you don't do it now, when will you do it?" It was as if he was looking inside me and, detecting a lack of courage, saw my excuse as invalid.

As years went on, more and more difficult decisions presented, and not unlike Hamlet's "To be or not to be," they presented new quandaries. To go or not to go, to stay or not to stay? And always there was a tempting easier way, but which way was the wisest? Was it the hardest or easiest? Was it God's way?

I soon observed there is always one good reason for not taking a proposed action. Often four good reasons may say "go," but one valid reason says "stay." It has happened so often that I can almost call it "Snyder's Rule." I was challenged when I came across Ecclesiastes 11:4: "He who observes the wind will not sow, and he who regards the clouds will not reap." In 1962 we were in London, with plans to embark for a fourteen-day ocean voyage to Durban, South Africa. One of our boys was sick with a "tummy ache." Was it beginning appendicitis? Would we be able to get medical care once on the trip? I examined his abdomen and determined it was not appendicitis at that moment, so unless it became definite we would stick with our plans. Hard decisions always look extra hard when making the wrong one could be disastrous. My mind can imagine all kinds of horrible outcomes.

"Just do it" could be horrible advice in many situations, but I think it is good advice when you are tempted to put off what your mind and heart tell you is the right thing to do. Ask yourself, "If I don't do it now, when will I do it? Am I just taking the easy way out?" Say to God, "My mind and heart tell me this is the right path. Others I trust agree. Your Word concurs." Then trust Providence by praying, "Sovereign God, this is what I plan to do. Please rule or overrule according to Your knowledge and plans for my life."

> "In his heart a man plans his course,
> but the Lord determines his steps."
> Prov. 16:9 NIV

Part Three:

God Is Love — A Great Discovery

My Journey into Light

In his book *Journey into Light*, theologian Emile Cailliet recounts events that led him, a pagan who never had seen a Bible, into the life of a believer. My journey into light was from a joyless Christian living in bondage, fear, and legalism into a convinced son of God enjoying all the rights and privileges of the family and an awareness of the vast love of God. My journey was from servantship to sonship.

I cannot tell why it took me so long. Maybe I am a slow learner. I have never known whether I am at the low end of the smart people, or at the high end of the dumb people, but it took too long for the light of God's love to dawn in me.

First John 1:5 reads, "This is the message we have heard from him and declare to you: God is light; in him there is no darkness at all." And in 1 John 4:8, "Whoever does not love does not know God, because God is love." And again, in 1 John 4:16, "God is love." (All verses are NIV.)

Our concept of God's character is thought to be based on our perception of our own fathers. I don't wish to denigrate my dad. He was a very caring father who loved his kids intensely, but I did not know that until I was grown up. He had been the middle child in a family of nine kids. His dad was a poor cobbler. Dad made his way on his own. Buying his own clothes from the time he was nine, he paid his own way through college, which was interrupted by World War I and service in France. His family almost mocked him when he talked about medical school. But he fought his way up—a no-nonsense guy who became one of the leading orthopedic surgeons in Michigan and chief of staff at Butterworth Hospital. As a child I revered my father, but I also feared him. The nurses in the operating room were also afraid of Dr. Snyder.

I knew my mother's love was unconditional, but I did not feel the same about Dad's. When I was four years old my brother Art, who was five, and I pulled off a robbery. Noting an open basement window in a vacated house, we tore through the screen and crawled into the basement. Spotting a shallow box of nuts and bolts, we grabbed it, and made our escape through the same window. Mother found the box, investigated, and realized she had a couple of budding criminals in the family. She usually handled discipline problems on her own, but this, being a felony involving her sons, was more than she cared to adjudicate.

When Dad arrived home and learned of our crime, he sat us down and immediately dialed the police station. Art and I were terrified, crying and screaming, unaware that Dad had his finger on the disconnect bar, faking the call. We listened as he explained our crime to the police, screaming and sobbing as Dad asked them how long we would have to stay in jail.

"Will they be locked up behind bars? Will they have only bread and water to eat?" he asked.

It was a terrifying moment, but a glimmer of hope presented itself as he continued with, "If I give them a good whipping, do you think that would be enough?"

And of course the fictitious cop accepted this solution. And we gladly accepted the whipping, preferring to fall into the hands of our dad.

If my siblings and I were fussing while traveling, Dad would say, "Stop or I will let you out to walk home," often slowing the car as he said it. Usually this happened on long trips, when we had no idea how to get home. I never doubted that he meant it.

I also believed that if I were to sass him or be impudent, I would be put out of the family. Like so many of my generation, I never remember my father actually saying, "I love you." He had never heard such statements during his own childhood, and it would have been foreign to him. In later life I realized that he did indeed love me and would have done anything for me. Unfortunately, my concept of my heavenly Father was already formed.

Much preaching in my early years was spiced with fear and legalism, hell and punishment. I may have selectively heard that slant more than others, or I may have been too dense to comprehend all the positive aspects. My mother, reared in a preacher's family, brought a lot of legalistic baggage into her parenting. Ample warnings certainly exist against willfully trespassing God's laws, but I wish I had been taught a little more about grace!

So, I walked in legalistic darkness, terrified of doing anything that might be contrary to God's will or commands. And in this shadow I slouched along for years. God had unquestionably saved me, but I did not have any freedom or joy. How could I witness to others? I had no joy to share. My idea of salvation was that when I was saved, God, because of Jesus' death, wiped the slate clean. I then started all over. If I were to sin, the bargain was off. Unless I asked forgiveness immediately, salvation was canceled. It was like the game of Monopoly: "Go to jail. Go directly to jail. Do not pass Go. Do not collect $200." Spiritually, I was perpetually slipping on a banana peel or plucking the petals off a daisy in a "He loves me— He loves me not" kind of relationship.

You might say I believed in "eternal insecurity." But God, in whom there is no darkness at all, slowly led me into a concept of His love, His joy, His peace, and His *grace*!

And God, who does not like darkness at all, began to lead me out of my gloom in many and varied ways. A first glimmer came while I was overseas as a soldier in the Philippine Islands. I became a chaplain's assistant and was part of the permanent staff of a replacement depot. Here military officers transited on their way to permanent assignment. I was invited to bring a devotional to a group of army nurses. Meeting with them was an army WAC (Women's' Auxiliary Corps), an Italian lady named Hannah Compania. Older than the nurses, she had been gloriously saved some years before and was a shining example of a joyous, vibrant Christian. Something I said during my talk caused her to take me aside and talk to me about the joy of the Lord. She insisted that I get a book called *The Christian's Secret of a Happy Life* by Hannah Whitall Smith.

I pondered why she had talked to me as she did. What had she observed? Obviously, she observed a legalistic, joyless Christian. Some years later, back in the U.S., I did get the book, and as I read it I understood why she thought I needed it.

Many years later, on the mission field, I felt concern for our African Christians who did not seem to comprehend the importance of a strict Christian walk. It seemed to me they thought God was a kindly Santa Claus. I talked to some older missionaries, a British couple by the name of Peter and Elisabeth Guillebaud. They had worked in evangelism and revival efforts in Rwanda for years.

I made the statement, "I think we need to preach more hellfire and brimstone to these people. They take things too lightly. I think they need to have more preaching on hell and punishment."

Immediately, Peter countered with, "Oh no! These people need to know about God's love. They live in fear of demons, ancestors, and all kinds of terrors haunt them." His words burned into my heart. "They need to know about God's love. They have never known love!"

Speaking to our hospital staff at morning prayers one day, I talked about love from 1 Corinthians 13:4-8: "Love is patient, love is kind. It does not envy, it does not boast, it is not proud. It is not rude, it is not self-seeking, it is not easily angered, it keeps no record of wrongs. Love does not delight in evil but rejoices with the truth. It always protects, always trusts, always hopes, always perseveres. Love never fails" (NIV). Then I finished with 1 John 4:16: "God is love."

I walked away with my own words speaking to me. I kept thinking, "If that is what love is, and God is love, that means that description of love is also a description of God. Certainly, God would not ask me to put all those attributes into my own life if He were not like that Himself."

My concept of God grew as I began to understand my father better and after becoming a father myself. When one of my brothers was finishing high school, he went through some emotional turmoil, which today we would probably call depression. My parents were at their wits' end trying to help him. Dad was just at the peak of his career, both in fame and fortune, when he said to Mother, "I would give everything I have if he would only get better." Another time, Louise and I, with our four boys, had come home from Africa and were staying with my parents when a terrible windstorm, with thunder and lightening, racked the house. The next day Mom recounted to me that as Dad had been up closing the windows, looking out at the storm, he said to her, "Oh, I am so glad they are all here safe under our roof!" As time went on, I began to realize that Dad would do anything for his kids.

In 1956, while living in Brussels and studying French, our eldest, seven-year-old Glenn, developed an illness that I felt was more than the virus a local pediatrician had diagnosed. I wondered if it might even be a surgical condition. (Eventually, it was diagnosed as acute glomerulonephritis, a kidney disorder.) We had friends who were U.S. Air Force pilots and frequently flew to the PX at Wiesbaden, Germany, to fulfill their required hours of flying. I phoned one of them for help. He said, "I'll call some buddies and see if I can get a crew together."

An hour later he phoned back to say, "I can't locate enough guys to fly, but my wife and I will drive you to Germany."

The following morning, after an all-night drive, we arrived bleary-eyed at the army hospital at Wiesbaden. They admitted Glenn to the pediatric ward to be seen by their doctors on morning rounds. I went to the PX and bought some things to keep Glenn entertained.

When I returned, I was told, "Sorry, no parents are allowed in our pediatric wards."

Almost pushing my way in, I insisted, "I must see him! I promised him I would be back. He does not know where I am staying. He has to have me explain it to him. We don't even live in Germany."

They relented, saying, "Okay, but just for one minute."

I found the doctors and nurses on rounds and at his bedside. I interrupted long enough to explain where I would be. I gave Glenn several things, including a drawing book.

As I started to leave, his lips quivered and his voice cracked as he said, "But Daddy, I don't have a pencil."

Immediately, several pencils appeared from the pockets of the surrounding medical team, as if that were a solution for a seven-year-old, sick and alone in a foreign country.

I turned and walked out, swallowing hard and trying to remain dry-eyed. A medical school classmate was living nearby. I contacted him and was invited to his house. Having been up all night, I crawled into bed, turned my head to the wall. Alone in Germany, with my son sick with who knew what, I sobbed my heart out.

I learned more of parental love over the years, as we suffered with our children. If they were happy, Louise and I were happy. If they were struggling, we felt it. We would make sure we were available. Often, we would stay near the phone, keeping the line free just to be there should they call.

Thinking about this I began to ask myself, "Is God like that? Is He sitting by ready to listen, to hear, to help?"

This was an epiphany for me as I realized that God *is* like that. He is standing nearby, ready to help. He does suffer when I suffer. Wasn't the first song I ever learned, "Jesus loves me, this I know, For the Bible tells me so?" Why had it taken me so long to comprehend it?

Jesus tells us of a father's love in the Parable of the Prodigal Son. Returning home filthy, smelling like pigs (probably the most repugnant of odors to a Jew), asking only to be a servant, and what does he find? A welcoming father looking down the path, overjoyed to see his son come home!

Jesus says in Matthew 7:11, "If you...though you are evil, know how to give good gifts to your children, how much more will your Father in heaven give good gifts to those who ask him!" (NIV).

Another Scripture that suddenly struck me late in life, like a flashbulb going off, is Romans 5:10, "For if, when we were God's enemies, we were reconciled to him through the death of his son, how much more, having been reconciled, shall we be saved through his life" (NIV). Reflecting upon this, I could not believe the implications of what it said. My interpretation as I understood this was that if while I was not even friendly to God, did not want to follow Him, and was an actual enemy, He drew me to Himself, how much more now that I want to be His follower, will He love, forgive, justify, and sustain me!

Finally, the immensity of God's love began to sink in, and I began to resonate with a hymn Charles Wesley wrote:

> Long my imprisoned spirit lay
> Fast bound in sin and nature's night.
> Thine eye diffused a quick'ning ray:
> I woke—the dungeon flamed with light!
> My chains fell off, my heart was free,
> I rose, went forth, and followed Thee.

"There is no fear in love; but perfect love casts out fear, because fear involves torment. But he who fears has not been made perfect in love," according to 1 John 4:18. A footnote in the Wesley Bible, comments on this: "Perfect love for God transforms our relationship to Him. Because we are living in love, just as God is love we are sure that on the Day of Judgment we will not be punished. We no longer fear His punishment but rather rest in His love (verses 17-19)."[6]

Unshackled from legalism and senseless scrupulosity, I began to feel the joy of the Lord and a desire to share the good news with others. I was for the first time experiencing freedom. An exhilaration bubbled up inside me, and I felt like a schoolboy walking outside on a balmy spring day, realizing school was out for the summer. Or maybe more like a prisoner being freed after hearing, "The court has found you not guilty!"

Biography

C. Albert Snyder earned his M.D. degree at the University of Michigan and trained in general surgery at Butterworth Hospital (now Spectrum Health) in Grand Rapids, Michigan. He is a fellow of the American College of Surgeons, is certified by the American Board of Surgery, and received a diploma in tropical medicine in Antwerp, Belgium. He was ordained a minister by the Rwanda General Conference of the Free Methodist Church. Al and his wife, Louise, have four sons (all of whom have worked or are working in Africa), and eight grandchildren.

Al is the author of On a Hill Far Away: Journal of a Missionary Doctor in Rwanda.

Endnotes

[1] C. Albert Snyder, On A Hill Far Away, Light and Life Communications 1995, pp. 46-49.

[2] Jerry Bridges, The Pursuit of Holiness, NavPress 1978, p. 81.

[3] L.E. Maxwell, Crowded to Christ, Wm. B. Eerdmans Publishing Co. 1950, p. 60.

[4] Oswald Chambers/James Reimann, ed. My Utmost for His Highest (Grand Rapids: Discovery House, 1992), November 16.

[5] Robert Frost, Complete Poems of Robert Frost, edited by Edward Comery Lathem, Henry Holt & Co NY, 1916.

[6] The Wesley Bible, NKJV. (Nashville: Thomas Nelson, 1990), footnote p.1897.

Printed in the United States
61402LVS00002B/190-258

9 781600 340154